D1095338

The Alternative Society

The Alternative Society

Essays From the Other World

Kenneth Rexroth

An *Azimuth* Book
Herder and Herder

1970
HERDER AND HERDER
232 Madison Avenue, New York 10016

The author extends grateful acknowledgement of the following periodicals, where chapters of this book originally appeared: *New World Writing* and New American Library for "Disengagement: The Art of the Beat Generation." *Jubilee* for "Morals, Ethics, Religion, Ideology, the Poet, Poetry." *The Nation* for "Black Writers—Black or White Readers." *Book Week* and the *New York Herald Tribune* for "Urbanism." *Holiday* for "Poetry in 1965." *Arts in Society* for "Why Is American Poetry Culturally Deprived?" *Harper's* for "Poetry and Money." *Playboy* for "The Heat." The *San Francisco Bay Guardian* for "The Demagogic Process." *Probe* for "Facing Extinction." "Community Planning" appeared as the Introduction to Sergius I. Chermayeff and C. Alexander, *Community and Privacy,* published in 1964 by Peter Smith. "The Second Post-War, the Second Interbellum, the Permanent War Generation" were written for the British Broadcasting Company.

Library of Congress Catalog Card Number: 71–116141

Manufactured in the United States

Contents

For Carol

The Alternative Society

1. Disengagement: The Art of the Beat Generation

Literature generally, but literary criticism in particular, has always been an area in which social forces assume symbolic guise, and work out—or at least exemplify—conflicts taking place in the contemporary, or rather, usually the just past, wider arena of society. Recognition of this does not imply the acceptance of any general theory of social or economic determinism. It is a simple, empirical fact. Because of the pervasiveness of consent in American society generally, that democratic leveling up or down so often bewailed since de Tocqueville, American literature, especially literary criticism, has usually been ruled by a "line." The fact that it was spontaneously evolved and enforced only by widespread consent has never detracted from its rigor—but rather the opposite. It is only human to kick against the prodding of a Leopold Auerbach or an Andrey Zhdanov. An invisible, all-enveloping compulsion is not likely to be recognized, let alone protested against.

After World War I there was an official line for general consumption: "Back to Normalcy." Day by day in every way, we are getting better and better. This produced a literature which tirelessly pointed out that there was nothing whatsoever normal about us. The measure of decay in thirty years is the degree of acceptance of the official myth today—from the most obscure hack on a provincial newspaper to the loftiest metaphysicians of the literary quarterlies. The line goes: "The generation of experimentation and revolt is over." This is an etherealized corollary of the general line: "The bull market will never end."

I do not wish to argue about the bull market, but in the arts nothing could be less true. The youngest generation is in a state of revolt so absolute that its elders cannot even recognize it. The disaffiliation, alienation, and rejection of the young has, as far as their elders are concerned, moved out of the visible spectrum altogether. Critically invisible, modern revolt, like X-rays and radioactivity, is perceived only by its effects at more materialistic social levels, where it is called delinquency.

"Disaffiliation," by the way, is the term used by the critic and poet, Lawrence Lipton, who has written several articles on this subject, the first of which, in the *Nation,* quoted as epigraph, "We disaffiliate . . ."—John L. Lewis.

Like the pillars of Hercules, like two ruined Titans guarding the entrance to one of Dante's circles, stand two great dead juvenile delinquents—the heroes of the post-war generation: the saxophonist, Charlie Parker, and Dylan Thomas. If the word "deliberate" means anything, both of them certainly deliberately destroyed themselves.

Both of them were overcome by the horror of the world in which they found themselves, because at last they could no longer overcome that world with the weapon of a purely lyrical art. Both of them were my friends. Living in San Francisco I saw them seldom enough to see them with a perspective which was not distorted by exasperation or fatigue. So as the years passed, I saw them each time in the light of an accelerated personal conflagration.

The last time I saw Bird, at Jimbo's Bob City, he was so gone —so blind to the world—that he literally sat down on me before he realized I was there. "What happened, man?" I said, referring to the pretentious "Jazz Concert." "Evil, man, evil," he said, and that's all he said for the rest of the night. About dawn he got up to blow. The rowdy crowd chilled into stillness and the fluent melody spiraled through it.

The last time I saw Dylan, his self-destruction had not just passed the limits of rationality. It had assumed the terrifying inertia of inanimate matter. Being with him was like being swept away by a torrent of falling stones.

Now Dylan Thomas and Charlie Parker have a great deal more in common than the same disastrous end. As artists, they were very similar. They were both very fluent. But this fluent, enchanting utterance had, compared with important artists of the past, relatively little content. Neither of them got very far beyond a sort of entranced rapture at his own creativity. The principal theme of Thomas's poetry was the ambivalence of birth and death—the pain of blood-stained creation. Music, of course, is not so explicit an art, but anybody who knew Charlie Parker knows that he felt much the same way about his own gift. Both of them did communicate one central theme: Against the ruin of the world, there is only one defense—the creative act. This, of course, is the theme of much art—perhaps most poetry. It is the theme of Horace, who certainly otherwise bears little resemblance to Parker or Thomas. The difference is that Horace accepted his theme with a kind of silken assurance. To Dylan and Bird it was an agony and terror. I do not believe that this is due to anything especially frightful about their relationship to their own creativity. I believe rather that it is due to the catastrophic world in which that creativity seemed to be the sole value. Horace's column of imperishable verse shines quietly enough in the lucid air of Augustan Rome. Art may have been for him the most enduring, orderly, and noble activity of man. But the other activities of his life partook of these values. They did not actively negate them. Dylan Thomas's verse had to find endurance in a world of burning cities and burning Jews. He was able to find meaning in his art as long as it was the answer to air raids and gas ovens. As the world began to take on the guise of an immense air raid or gas oven, I believe his art became meaningless to him. I think all this could apply to Parker just as well, although, because of the nature of music, it is not demonstrable—at least not conclusively.

Thomas and Parker have more in common than theme, attitude, life pattern. In the practice of their art, there is an obvious technical resemblance. Contrary to popular belief, they were not great technical innovators. Their effects are only superficially startling. Thomas is a regression from the technical originality and ingenuity of writers like Pierre Reverdy or Apollinaire. Similarly, the innovations of bop, and of Parker particularly, have been vastly overrated by people unfamiliar with music, especially by that ignoramus, the intellectual jitterbug, the jazz aficionado. The tonal novelties consist in the introduction of a few chords used in classical music for centuries. And there is less rhythmic difference between progressive jazz, no matter how progressive, and Dixieland, than there is between two movements of many conventional symphonies.

What Parker and his contemporaries—Gillespie, Davis, Monk, Roach (Tristano is an anomaly), etc.—did was to absorb the musical ornamentation of older jazz into the basic structure, of which it then became an integral part, and with which it then developed. This is true of the melodic line which could be put together from selected passages of almost anybody—Benny Carter, Johnny Hodges. It is true of the rhythmic pattern in which the beat shifts continuously, or at least is continuously sprung, so that it becomes ambiguous enough to allow the pattern to be dominated by the long pulsations of the phrase or strophe. This is exactly what happened in the transition from baroque to rococo music. It is the difference between Bach and Mozart.

It is not a farfetched analogy to say that this is what Thomas did to poetry. The special syntactical effects of a Rimbaud or an Edith Sitwell—actually ornaments—become the main concern. The metaphysical conceits, which fascinate the Reactionary Generation still dominant in backwater American colleges, were embroideries. Thomas's ellipses and ambiguities are ends in themselves. The immediate theme, if it exists, is incidental, and his main theme—the terror of birth—is simply reiterated.

This is one difference between Bird and Dylan which should be pointed out. Again, contrary to popular belief, there is nothing crazy or frantic about Parker either musically or emotionally. His sinuous melody is a sort of naïve transcendence of all experience. Emotionally, it does not resemble Berlioz or Wagner; it resembles Mozart. This is true also of a painter like Jackson Pollock. He may have been eccentric in his behavior, but his paintings are as impassive as Persian tiles. Partly this difference is due to the nature of verbal communication. The insistent talk-aboutiveness of the general environment obtrudes into even the most idyllic poetry. It is much more a personal difference. Thomas certainly wanted to tell people about the ruin and disorder of the world. Parker and Pollock wanted to substitute a work of art for the world.

Technique pure and simple, rendition, is not of major importance, but it is interesting that Parker, following Lester Young, was one of the leaders of the so-called saxophone revolution. In modern jazz, the saxophone is treated as a woodwind and played with conventional embouchure. Metrically, Thomas's verse was extremely conventional, as was, incidentally, the verse of that other tragic enragé, Hart Crane.

I want to make clear what I consider the one technical development in the first wave of significant post-war arts. Ornament is confabulation in the interstices of structure. A poem by Dylan Thomas, a saxophone solo by Charles Parker, a painting by Jackson Pollock—these are pure confabulations as ends in themselves. Confabulation has come to determine structure. Uninhibited lyricism should be distinguished from its exact opposite—the sterile, extraneous invention of the corn-belt metaphysicals, our present blight of poetic professors.

Just as Hart Crane had little influence on anyone except very reactionary writers—like Allen Tate, for instance, to whom Valéry was the last word in modern poetry and the felicities of an Apollinaire, let alone a Paul Éluard, were nonsense—so Dylan Thomas's influence has been slight indeed. In fact, his only disciple—the only person to imitate his style—was W. S. Graham, who seems to have imitated him without much understanding, and who has since moved on to other methods. Thomas's principle influence lay in the communication of an attitude—that of the now extinct British romantic school of the New Apocalypse—Henry Treece, J. F. Hendry, and others—all of whom were quite conventional poets.

Parker certainly had much more of an influence. At one time it was the ambition of every saxophone player in every high school band in America to blow like Bird. Even before his death this influence had begun to ebb. In fact, the whole generation of the founding fathers of bop—Gillespie, Monk, Davis, Blakey, and the rest—are just now at a considerable discount. The main line of development today goes back to Lester Young and bypasses them.

The point is that many of the most impressive developments in the arts nowadays are aberrant, idiosyncratic. There is no longer any sense of continuing development of the sort that can be traced from Baudelaire to Éluard, or for that matter from Hawthorne through Henry James to Gertrude Stein. The cubist generation before World War I, and, on a lower level, the surrealists of the period between the wars, both assumed an accepted universe of discourse, in which, to quote André Breton, it was possible to make definite advances, exactly as in the sciences. I doubt if anyone holds such ideas today. Continuity exists, but like the neo-swing music developed from Lester Young, it is a continuity sustained by popular demand.

In the plastic arts, a very similar situation exists. Surrealists like Hans Arp and Max Ernst might talk of creation by hazard—of composing pictures by walking on them with painted soles, or by tossing bits of paper up in the air. But it is obvious that they were self-deluded. Nothing looks anything like an Ernst or an Arp but another Ernst or Arp. Nothing looks less like their work than the happenings of random occasion. Many of the post-World War II abstract expressionists, apostles of the discipline of spontaneity and hazard, look alike, and do look like accidents. The aesthetic appeal of pure paint laid on at random may exist, but it is a very impoverished appeal. Once again what has happened is an all-consuming confabulation of the incidentals, the accidents of painting. It is curious that at its best, the work of this school of painting—Mark Rothko, Jackson Pollock, Clyfford Still, Robert Motherwell, William deKooning, and the rest—resembles nothing so much as the passage painting of quite unimpressive painters: the mother-of-pearl shimmer in the background of a Henry McFee, itself a formula derived from Renoir; the splashes of light and black which fake drapery in the fashionable imitators of Hals and Sargent. Often work of this sort is presented as calligraphy—the pure utterance of the brush stroke seeking only absolute painteresque values. You have only to compare such painting with the work of, say, Sesshu, to realize that someone is using words and brushes carelessly.

At its best the abstract expressionists achieve a simple rococo decorative surface. Its poverty shows up immediately when compared with Tiepolo, where the rococo rises to painting of extraordinary profundity and power. A Tiepolo painting, however confabulated, is a universe of tensions in vast depths. A Pollock is an object of art—bijouterie—disguised only by its great size. In fact, once the size is big enough to cover a whole wall, it turns into nothing more than extremely expensive wallpaper. Now there is nothing wrong with complicated wallpaper. There is just more to Tiepolo. The great Ashikaga brush painters painted wallpapers, too—at least portable ones, screens.

A process of elimination which leaves the artist with nothing but the play of his materials themselves cannot sustain interest in either artist or public for very long. So in recent years abstract expressionism has tended towards romantic suggestion—indications of landscape or living figures. This approaches the work of the Northwest school—Clayton Price, Mark Tobey, Kenneth Callahan, Morris Graves—who have of all recent painters come nearest to conquering a territory which painting could occupy with some degree of security. The Northwest school, of course, admittedly is influenced by the ink painters of the Far East, and by Tintoretto and Tiepolo. The dominant school of post-World War II American painting has really been a long detour into plastic nihilism. I should add that painters like Ernie Briggs seem to be opening up new areas of considerable scope within the main traditional abstract expressionism—but with remarkable convergence to Tobey or Tintoretto, as you prefer.

Today American painting is just beginning to emerge with a transvaluation of values. From the mid-nineteenth century on, all ruling standards in the plastic arts were subject to continual attack. They were attacked because each on-coming generation had new standards of its own to put in their place. Unfortunately, after one hundred years of this, there grew up a generation ignorant of the reasons for the revolt of their elders, and without any standards whatever. It has been necessary to create standards anew out of chaos. This is what modern education purports to do with finger painting in nursery schools. This is why the Northwest school has enjoyed such an advantage over the abstract expressionists. Learning by doing, by trial and error, is learning by the hardest way. If you want to overthrow the cubist tradition of architectural painting, it is much easier to seek out its opposites in the history of culture and study them carefully. At least it saves a great deal of time.

One thing can be said of painting in recent years—its revolt, its rejection of the classic modernism of the first half of the century, has been more absolute than in any other art. The only ancestor of abstract expressionism is the early Kandinsky—a style rejected even by Kandinsky himself. The only painter in a hundred years who bears the slightest resemblance to Tobey or Graves is Odilon Redon (perhaps Gustave Moreau a little), whose stock was certainly not very high with painters raised in the cubist tradition.

The ready market for prose fiction has had a decisive influence on its development. Sidemen with Kenton or Herman may make a good if somewhat hectic living, but any novelist who can write home to mother, or even spell his own name, has a chance to become another Brubeck. The deliberately and painfully intellectual fiction which appears in the literary quarterlies is a by-product of certain classrooms. The only significant fiction in America is popular fiction. Nobody realizes this better than the French. To them our late-born imitators of Henry James and E. M. Forster are just *chiens qui fument,* and arithmetical horses and bicycling seals. And there is no more perishable commodity than the middle-brow novel. No one today reads Ethel L. Voynich or Joseph Hergesheimer, just as no one in the future will read the writers' workshop pupils and teachers who fill the literary quarterlies. Very few people, except themselves, read them now.

On the other hand, the connection between the genuine high-brow writer and the genuinely popular is very close. Hemingway had hardly started to write before his style had been reduced to a formula in *Black Mask,* the first hard-boiled detective magazine. In no time at all he had produced two first-class popular writers, Raymond Chandler and Dashiell Hammett. Van Vechten, their middle-brow contemporary, is forgotten. It is from Chandler and Hammett and Hemingway that the best modern fiction derives; although most of it comes out in hard covers, it is always thought of as written for a typical pocketbook audience. Once it gets into pocketbooks it is sometimes difficult to draw the line between it and its most ephemeral imitators. Even the most *précieux* French critics, a few years ago, considered Horace McCoy America's greatest contemporary novelist. There is not only something to be said for their point of view; the only thing to be said against it is that they don't read English.

Much of the best popular fiction deals with the world of the utterly disaffiliated. Burlesque and carnival people, hipsters, handicappers and hop heads, wanted men on the lam, an expendable squad of soldiers being expended, anyone who by definition is divorced from society and cannot afford to believe even an iota of the social lie—these are the favorite characters of modern postwar fiction, from Norman Mailer to the latest ephemerid called *Caught,* or *Hung Up,* or *The Needle,* its bright cover winking invitingly in the drugstore. The first, and still the greatest, novelist of total disengagement is not a young man at all, but an elderly former I.W.W. of Germany ancestry, B. Traven, the author of *The Death Ship* and *The Treasure of Sierra Madre.*

It is impossible for an artist to remain true to himself as a man, let alone an artist, and work within the context of this society. Contemporary mimics of Jane Austen or Anthony Trollope are not only beneath contempt. They are literally unreadable. It is impossible to keep your eyes focused on the page. Writers as far apart as J. F. Powers and Nelson Algren agree in one thing—their diagnosis of an absolute corruption.

This refusal to accept the mythology of press and pulpit as a medium for artistic creation, or even enjoyable reading matter, is one explanation for the popularity of escapist literature. Westerns, detective stories, and science fiction are all situated beyond the pale of normal living. The slick magazines are only too well aware of this, and in these three fields especially exert steady pressure on their authors to accentuate the up-beat. The most shocking example of this forced perversion is the homey science-fiction story, usually written by a woman, in which a one-to-one correlation has been made for the commodity-ridden tale of domestic whimsey, the stand-by of magazines given away in the chain groceries. In writers like Judith Merrill the space pilot and his bride bat the badinage back and forth while the robot maid makes breakfast in the jet-propelled lucite orange squeezer and the electronic bacon rotobroiler, dropping pearls of dry assembly plant wisdom (like plantation wisdom but drier), the whilst. Still, few yield to these pressures, for the obvious reason that fiction indistinguishable from the advertising columns on either side of the page defeats its own purpose, which is to get the reader to turn over the pages when he is told "continued on p. 47."

Simenon is still an incomparably better artist and psychologist than the psychological Jean Stafford. Ward Moore is a better artist than Eudora Welty, and Ernest Haycox than William Faulkner, just as, long ago, H. G. Wells was a better artist, as artist, than E. M. Forster, as well as being a lot more interesting. At its best, popular literature of this sort, coming up, meets high-brow literature coming down. It has been apparent novel by novel that Nelson Algren is rising qualitatively in this way. In *A Walk on the Wild Side,* thoroughly popular in its materials, he meets and absorbs influences coming down from the top, from the small handful of bona fide high-brow writers working today—Céline, Jean Genêt, Samuel Beckett, Henry Miller. In Algren's case this has been a slow growth, and he has carried his audience with him. Whatever the merits of his subject matter or his thesis—"It is better to be out than in. It is better to be on the lam than on the cover of *Time* Magazine"—his style started out as a distressing mixture of James Farrell and Kenneth Fearing. Only later did he achieve an idiom of his own.

There is only one thing wrong with this picture, and that is that the high-brow stimulus still has to be imported. Algren, who is coming to write more and more like Céline, has no difficulty selling his fiction. On the other hand, an author like Jack Kerouac, who is in his small way the peer of Céline, Destouches, or Beckett, is the most famous "unpublished" author in America. Every publisher's reader and adviser of any moment has read him and was enthusiastic about him. In other words, anybody emerging from the popular field has every advantage. It is still extremely difficult to enter American fiction from the top down.

The important point about modern fiction is that it is salable, and therefore negotiable in our society, and therefore successful in the best sense of the word. When a novelist has something to say, he knows people will listen. Only the jazz musician, but to a much lesser degree, shares this confidence in his audience. It is of the greatest social significance that the novelists who say, "I am proud to be delinquent" are sold in editions of hundreds of thousands.

Nobody much buys poetry. I know. I am one of the country's most successful poets. My books actually sell out—in editions of two thousand. Many a poet, the prestige ornament of a publisher's list, has more charges against his royalty account than credits for books sold. The problem of poetry is the problem of communication itself. All art is a symbolic criticism of values, but poetry is specifically and almost exclusively that. A painting decorates the wall. A novel is a story. Music . . . soothes a savage breast. But poetry you have to take straight. In addition, the entire educational system is in a conspiracy to make poetry as unpalatable as possible. From the seventh-grade teacher who rolls her eyes and chants H. D. to the seven types of ambiguity factories, grinding out little Donnes and Hopkinses with hayseeds in their hair, everybody is out to de-poetize forever the youth of the land. Again, bad and spurious painting, music, and fiction are not really well-organized, except on obvious commercial levels, where they can be avoided. But in poetry Gresham's Law is supported by the full weight of the powers that be. From about 1930 on, a conspiracy of bad poetry has been as carefully organized as the Communist Party, and today controls most channels of publication except the littlest of the little magazines. In all other departments of American culture, English influence has been at a steadily declining minimum since the middle of the nineteenth century. In 1929, this was still true of American poetry. Amy Lowell, Sandburg, H. D., Pound, Marianne Moore, William Carlos Williams, Wallace Stevens—all of the major poets of the first quarter of the century owed far more to Apollinaire or Francis Jammes than they did to the whole body of the English tradition. In fact, the new poetry was essentially an anti-English, pro-French movement—a provincial but clear echo of the French revolt against the symbolists. On the other hand, Jules Laforgue and his English disciples, Ernest

Dowson and Arthur Symons, were the major influence on T. S. Eliot. Unfortunately Mr. Eliot's poetic practice and his thoroughly snobbish critical essays which owed their great cogency to their assumption, usually correct, that his readers had never heard of the authors he discussed—Webster, Crashaw, or Lancelot Andrewes—lent themselves all too easily to the construction of an academy and the production of an infinite number of provincial academicians—policemen entrusted with the enforcement of Gresham's Law.

Behind the façade of this literary Potemkin village, the mainstream of American poetry, with its sources in Baudelaire, Lautréamont, Rimbaud, Apollinaire, Jammes, Reverdy, Salmon, and later Breton and Éluard, has flowed on unperturbed, though visible only at rare intervals between the interstices of the academic hoax. Today the class magazines and the quarterlies are filled with poets as alike as two bad pennies. It is my opinion that these people do not really exist. Most of them are androids designed by Ransom, Tate, and Co., and animated by Randall Jarrell. They are not just counterfeit; they are not even real counterfeits, but counterfeits of counterfeits. On these blurred and clumsy coins the lineaments of Mr. Eliot and I. A. Richards dimly can be discerned, like the barbarized Greek letters which nobody could read on Scythian money.

This is the world in which over every door is written the slogan: "The generation of experiment and revolt is over. Bohemia died in the Twenties. There are no more little magazines." Actually there have never been so many little magazines. In spite of the fantastic costs of printing, more people than ever are bringing out little sheets of free verse and making up the losses out of their own pockets. This world has its own major writers, its own discoveries, its own old masters, its own tradition and continuity. Its sources are practically exclusively French, and they are all post-symbolist, even anti-symbolist. It is the Reactionary Generation who are influenced by Laforgue, the symbolists, and Valéry. Nothing is more impressive than the strength, or at least the cohesion, of this underground movement. Poets whom the quarterlies pretend never existed, like Louis Zukovsky and Jack Wheelwright, are still searched out in large libraries or obscure bookshops and copied into notebooks by young writers. I myself have a complete typewritten collection of the pre-reactionary verse of Yvor Winters. And I know several similar collections of "forgotten modernists" in the libraries of my younger friends. People are always turning up who say something like, "I just discovered a second-hand copy of Parker Tyler's *The Granite Butterfly* in a Village bookshop. It's great, man." On the other hand, I seriously doubt whether *The Hudson Review* would ever consider for a moment publishing a line of Parker Tyler's verse. And he is certainly not held up as an example in the Iowa Writers' Workshop. There are others who have disappeared entirely—Charles Snider, Sherry Mangan, R. E. F. Larsson, the early Winters, the last poems of Ford Madox Ford. They get back into circulation, as far as I know, only when I read them to somebody at home or on the air, and then I am always asked for a copy. Some of the old avant-garde seem to have written themselves out, for instance, Mina Loy. There are a few established old masters, outstanding of whom are, of course, Ezra Pound and William Carlos Williams. I am not a passionate devotee of Pound myself. In fact, I think his influence is largely pernicious. But no one could deny its extent and power amongst young people today. As for Williams, more and more people, even some of the Reactionary Generation, have come to think of him as our greatest living poet. Even Randall Jarrell and R. P. Blackmur have good words to say for him.

Then there is a middle generation which includes Kenneth Patchen, Jean Garrigue, myself, and a few others—notably Richard Eberhart, who looks superficially as if he belonged with the Tates and Blackmurs but who is redeemed by his directness, simplicity, and honesty; and Robert Fitzgerald and Dudley Fitts. Curiously enough, in the taste of the young, Kenneth Fearing is not included in this group, possibly because his verse is too easy. It does include the major work, for example, *Ajanta,* of Muriel Rukeyser.

I should say that the most influential poets of the youngest established generation of the avant-garde are Denise Levertov, Robert Creeley, Charles Olson, Robert Duncan, and Philip Lamantia. The most influential avant-garde editor is perhaps Cid Corman, with his magazine *Origin.* Richard Emerson's

Golden Goose and Robert Creeley's *Black Mountain Review* seem to have suspended publication temporarily. Jonathan Williams, himself a fine poet, publishes the Jargon Press.

All of this youngest group have a good deal in common. They are all more or less influenced by French poetry, and by Céline, Beckett, Artaud, Genêt, to varying degrees. They are also influenced by William Carlos Williams, D. H. Lawrence, Whitman, Pound. They are all interested in Far Eastern art and religion; some even call themselves Buddhists. Politically they are all strong disbelievers in the State, war, and the values of commercial civilization. Most of them would no longer call themselves anarchists, but just because adopting such a label would imply adherence to a "movement." Anything in the way of an explicit ideology is suspect. Contrary to gossip of a few years back, I have never met anybody in this circle who was a devotée of the dubious notions of the psychologist Wilhelm Reich; in fact, few of them have ever read him, and those who have consider him a charlatan.

Although there is wide diversity—Olson is very like Pound; Creeley resembles Mallarmé; Denise Levertov in England was a leading New Romantic, in America she came under the influence of William Carlos Williams; Robert Duncan has assimilated ancestors as unlike as Gertrude Stein and Éluard, and so on—although this diversity is very marked, there is a strong bond of esthetic unity too. No avant-garde American poet accepts the I. A. Richards-Valéry thesis that a poem is an end in itself, an anonymous machine for providing esthetic experiences. All believe in poetry as communication, statement from one person to another. So they all avoid the studied ambiguities and metaphysical word play of the Reactionary Generation and seek clarity of image and simplicity of language.

In the years since the war, it would seem as though more and more of what is left of the avant-garde has migrated to Northern California. John Berryman once referred to the Lawrence cult of "mindless California," and Henry Miller and I have received other unfavorable publicity which has served only to attract people to this area. Mr. Karl Shapiro, for instance, once referred to San Francisco as "the last refuge of the bohemian remnant" —a description he thought of as invidious. Nevertheless it is true that San Francisco is today the seat of an intense literary activity not unlike Chicago of the first quarter of the century. A whole school of poets has grown up—almost all of them migrated here from somewhere else. Some of them have national reputations, at least in limited circles. For example, Philip Lamantia among the surrealists; William Everson (Brother Antoninus, O.P.)—perhaps the best Catholic poet. Others have come up, like Lawrence Ferlinghetti, Allen Ginsberg, Gary Snyder, Philip Whalen, David Meltzer, Michael McClure, still have largely local reputations. But the strength of these reputations should not be underestimated. The Poetry Center of San Francisco State College, directed by Ruth Witt-Diamant, gives a reading to a large audience at least twice a month. And there are other readings equally well attended every week in various galleries and private homes.

This means that poetry has become an actual social force—something which has always sounded hitherto like a Utopian dream of the William Morris sort. It is a very thrilling experience to hear an audience of more than three hundred people stand and cheer and clap, as they invariably do at a reading by Allen Ginsberg, certainly a poet of revolt if there ever was one.

There is no question but that the San Francisco renaissance is radically different from what is going on elsewhere. There are hand presses, poetry readings, young writers elsewhere—but nowhere else is there a whole younger generation culture pattern characterized by total rejection of the official high-brow culture —where critics like John Crowe Ransom or Lionel Trilling, magazines like the *Kenyon, Hudson* and *Partisan* reviews, are looked on as "The Enemy"—the other side of the barricades.

There is only one trouble about the renaissance in San Francisco. It is too far away from the literary market place. That, of course, is the reason why the bohemian remnant, the avant-garde have migrated here. It is possible to hear the story about what so-and-so said to someone else at a cocktail party twenty years ago just one too many times. You grab a plane or get on your thumb and hitchhike to the other side of the continent for good and all. Each generation, the great Latin poets came from farther and farther from Rome. Eventually, they ceased even to go there except to see the sights.

Distance from New York City does, however, make it harder to get things, if not published, at least nationally circulated. I recently formed a collection for one of the foundations of avant-garde poetry printed in San Francisco. There were a great many items. The poetry was all at least readable, and the hand printing and binding were in most cases very fine indeed. None of these books was available in bookstores elsewhere in the country, and only a few of them had been reviewed in newspapers or magazines with national circulation.

Anyway, as an old war horse of the revolution of the word, things have never looked better from where I sit. The avant-garde has not only not ceased to exist. It's jumping all over the place. Something's happening, man.

The disengagement of the creator, who, as creator, is necessarily judge, is one thing, but the utter nihilism of the emptied-out hipster is another. What is going to come of an attitude like this? It is impossible to go on indefinitely saying: "I am proud to be a delinquent," without destroying all civilized values. Between such persons no true enduring interpersonal relationships can be built, and of course, nothing resembling a true "culture"—an at-homeness of men with each other, their work, their loves, their environment. The end result must be the desperation of shipwreck—the despair, the orgies, ultimately the cannibalism of a lost lifeboat. I believe that most of an entire generation will go to ruin—the ruin of Céline, Artaud, Rimbaud, voluntarily, even enthusiastically. What will happen afterwards I don't know, but for the next couple of decades we are going to have to cope with the youth that we, my generation, put through the atom smasher. Social disengagement, artistic integrity, voluntary poverty—these are powerful virtues and may pull them through, but they are not the virtues we tried to inculcate—rather they are the exact opposite.

Note: This was the launching gun, the finger removed from the dike. It was published in 1957 in "New World Writing." This book is a record of the vast changes since then.

2.

Morals, Ethics, Religion, Ideology, the Poet, Poetry

Dear Ned O'Gorman,
It seems to me that if I cast this essay into the form of a letter to you, answering directly your questions which you were good enough to send me as suggestions for an outline, this piece would have the merits of simplicity, directness, and a person-to-person approach to the reader. Certainly these are the virtues of the best prose under most any circumstances, and they are particularly desirable in dealing with this, the perennial subject of art and human responsibility.

Does the moral integrity of a poet affect his work? Does it exert an influence over it?

Of course it affects it. Anything a poet does which involves him at all deeply affects his work. There is no logical reason why good men should write good poems or bad men should write bad ones. However, the distinction between the artist and the man is only a logical one. Artists, poets, are men. All men have responsibilities as men before they have responsibilities as artists. If they do not fulfill them they weaken to just that degree their integrity as men. Essential to the ability to cope with life creatively is, more than anything else, personal integrity. Notorious evil-livers may have been great artists, but there is little doubt but that they would have been better artists if they had been better men.

The evil of the Great Sinners of literature is greatly overrated —not least by themselves. There aren't many. Petronius, Aretino, Rochester, Baudelaire, Wilde, there are thousands of politicians, kings, bankers, peasants, and plain men who could put them to shame. A bad life is very time-consuming and poetry is an onerous and time-consuming craft. Spiritual conflicts, crises of conscience, do not constitute lack of moral integrity, rather the opposite. So men like Baudelaire, Rochester, and Wilde are tragic figures rather than immoral men. Psychosis is not sin. So the Marquis de Sade is insane, not evil, and his blatantly "evil" writings are as dull as the ravings of any other lunatic. I should imagine that a thorough-going betrayal of one's own integrity would be crippling in every way, not least in the practice of an art.

Does adherence to a system of religious doctrines hamper the poet? Obviously not. It has not hampered Thomas Merton or Sister Madeleva or Brother Antonius or R. E. F. Larsson, or Daniel Berrigan, as it did not hamper Hopkins or Donne or Dante in the past. I can imagine, without great effort, a system of religious doctrines so outrageous and implausible that no one could make great poetry with them or out of them. There are a number of cults of what Toynbee calls the Internal Proletariat flourishing today that have never shown signs of producing a poet of any sort, though they number many thousands of adherents. Sophistication of doctrine, or even literacy, is not a test, as is shown by the great poetry of Negro Spirituals or certain hymns of the early years of the Reformation, or by St. Francis's *Hymn of the Sun.*

Does a poet's world view modify, affect, lessen, enlarge his work? Yes, if he has one. A great many poets have been a mite scant when it came to world view. True, we say that the poet has a vatic role in society, that he is called to the vocation of the Hebrew prophets. But this is a pious wish, not an empirical fact. History is full of charming poets who never had a major idea in their heads. Others, very great ones, like Horace, never rise above the level of an urbane newspaper columnist.

How do a poet's ideologies affect his work? It all depends on the poet, the ideology, and the circumstances. Allegiance to Marxism does not seem to have damaged the early work of Éluard, Neruda, or Louis Aragon. However, during the period of the Moscow Trials and the Hitler Stalin Pact it would be charitable to say that their poetry lacked a certain convincingness. Propaganda poetry, written to order for a political or religious institution, is really commercial art and should be judged by such standards.

What is the relationship of morality to the art of the poet in this society? "This society," as was pointed out by St. Paul, is not conspicuous for any morality. However, modern literary and artistic society tends to substitute art for religion. Much modern criticism places a burden on the artist that he was never designed to bear. On the other hand, modern social practice, rather than theory, has led to a radical divorce between the professional practice of religion and the practice of the arts. This is just part of the over-specialization of modern life. There is no reason why a saint or a theologian should not be a very great poet. St. Thomas and Abelard are the greatest poets of the Middle Ages —Adam of St. Victor, Robert Grossteste, Venantius Fortunatus —the list can be prolonged indefinitely. Dante was hardly a great theologian, but he was not an inconsiderable one. It would be very nice if this sort of thing were to come back into fashion.

What does modern morality in literature consist of? Which modern morality? Bernanos? Louis Aragon? Wallace Stevens? Paul Valéry? Robert Frost? All the moralities contending in modern life seem to have found their poets. If you mean what the critics of the nineteen hundreds called "the Modern Spirit," I suppose this means the utmost freedom of self-determination for the individual. The First War is supposed to have demonstrated to men of moral sensibility that this was inadequate as a general principle for civilized life. It is still very popular in commercially successful novels, but nowhere else.

1961

3.

Black Writers–Black or White Readers

Between August 5–9, 1964, at Asilomar, a conference camp on the forested shore of Monterey Bay, operated by the California State Parks under the auspices of the Letters and Science Extension, Special Programs of the University of California, and under the general management of Herbert Hill, Labor Secretary of the NAACP, there was held a conference on the Negro writer in the United States. About two hundred people attended as audience. There must have been some thirty representatives of the press and ten people gave speeches and led discussions —Arna Bontemps, Gwendolyn Brooks, Horace Cayton, LeRoi Jones, Saunders Redding, Ossie Davis, Nat Hentoff, Harvey Swados, Robert Bone, Herbert Hill. James Baldwin and Ralph Ellison were scheduled but cancelled their engagements. Juridically speaking, the affair was a summer-school course of the University of California. There were a few scholarships and the press representatives who paid only their board. Otherwise the audience paid one hundred dollars for tuition, board, and room.

The discussion leaders were transported across the country and were paid the usual fees for such appearances.

I have given you all these vital statistics because they are really more important than anything said at the conference. They are a most clear demonstration of what has become a characteristic social mechanism—the institutionalization of dissent and revolt. All of us with grey hair who were in this thing way back when can remember hitchhiking, riding freights, or struggling across the country in packed, periodically collapsing jalopies to meetings concerned with what on the face of it seemed to be the same problem. We slept on one another's floors; we kept going through the day on coffee and donuts; we quarrelled violently about art and politics, form and content, and were buffeted on one side by the cops and on the other side by the Apparatchiks. Today, Malcolm X is invited to address executive seminars at Shangri-las nestled in the snow-clad Rockies. We are all indulged rebels if we are not allowed clowns. In fact, indulgence hastes to anticipate rebellion. All you have to do nowadays is begin to growl and somebody in a pin-striped suit with real buttonholes on the cuffs shows up with a fist-full of foundation money.

Does it mean anything? Harlem gets catastrophically worse and worse by the second. Goon squads seize the Party of the Great Emancipator, while representatives of the State Department abuse the Black Bourgeoisie gathered in the conclave of the leading Negro Greek letter organization for their lack of militancy.

There was plenty of militancy at Asilomar. Meeting under the storm clouds of the nomination of Goldwater and the Harlem riots (which, as everybody was too excited to point out, have a very obvious connection), the conference kept turning into a civil-rights rally. Everybody tried to be as charismatic as he could be. This was not Herb Hill's fault. NAACP or no, he tried to keep the people talking about writing. The only genuinely literary discussions occurred in brief interchanges after the papers on Ellison, Baldwin, Toomer, and Wright, and they bore a chilly resemblance to the battles of the Thirties over form and content and Art and the Masses. Just like the John Reed Club or the League of American Writers, most of the wordage was spent offering up dense clouds of verbal incense on the altars of Our Great Writers, a commendable but unilluminating ritual.

Stars of the show were LeRoi Jones, Horace Cayton, and Ossie Davis. True, they talked about the problems of the Negro writer, but in general terms of moral exhortation. I have great respect for all three of these men. I know that they are, in fact, concerned with all sorts of concrete problems and their work is much broader and deeper and at the same time more pointed than propaganda and protest literature, but that was not the effect of their talks. Partly, this was due to audience response and speaker projection. You put 250 Negroes and whites together in an auditorium today and you get a civil-rights rally, willy-nilly. The three programs that raised a genuine literary response from the audience were the poetry readings by Gwendolyn Brooks and LeRoi Jones and Arna Bontemps' talk on Jean Toomer and the Harlem Renaissance. Gwendolyn Brooks' encores were a revelation to the whites in the audience. People obviously knew her work by heart and called again and again for one favorite poem after another. LeRoi Jones stands at the opposite pole of American literature and Negro life, yet the audience was at least as attentive and a number (that surprised even me) requested favorite poems. More remarkable, any attempt to create a literary antagonism or schism between Miss Brooks and Mr. Jones was fiercely resisted by ordinary people in the audience. This was not just "defending our own." It revealed a degree of understanding of how poetry works that would be unlikely in an all-white audience.

More surprising was the response, especially on the part of young people and especially the more militant and even hostile ones, to Arna Bontemps' talk. When he finished a forest of hands went up. Everybody wanted to know more about the legendary figures of Harlem's golden age and everybody wanted to discuss the spiritual and literary problems of a very great writer, almost certainly the greatest Negro writer up to this time, who had, for religious mystical reasons, rather than racial ones, long ago renounced both his race and literature. Most of them had never heard of him, but they certainly wanted to hear more. And I,

4. Community Planning

Every month enough human beings to make a city the size of Detroit are added to the world's population. In a few years it will be a city the size of Chicago—every single month. The annual growth of India's population is equal to the total population of Australia.

We are all aware of the population explosion, although with our present economy of abundance and our still uncrowded country, we are, most of us, only intellectually aware of it. And very few of us are aware of how rapidly its effects are being felt in many parts of the world. It is a pity that we can't travel in time and space and visit Madras and Canton and Java in 1850, in 1900, and today. Those of us who are old enough can at least compare life in our own cities, in Paris and London and New York, a generation ago and today.

Man creates his own environment—and at an accelerated pace. Create is hardly the word, so far he has simply made it, in the sense in which we say, "Well, you've made your bed, now you'll have to lie in it." It is obvious that it is on the verge, even in the richest and most highly developed countries, of getting beyond him.

Most speculation about the dangers of the population explosion are concerned with economic factors—especially with the dwindling food supply and the exhaustion of natural resources. There is another, graver danger, the aesthetic danger. This may sound frivolous to some, but indeed it is not. On the organic, physiological, neurological, emotional response of man to his environment depends his health as a species.

We make fun of the word "togetherness" but there is nothing funny about the increasing failure of our own togetherness with ourselves and the rest of life on this planet. Ecology is the science of the togetherness of living things and their environment. Man is so radically altering the ecological situation out of which he emerged as a species, and altering it in such an irrational manner that he is endangering his own future.

If in the next century the world grows to five billion people (and at present rates it will grow to far more than that), all living in a hundred thousand or more Calcuttas and Harlems, it may be possible to feed everybody on tanks of algae in the cities, the farming of the sea, the synthesization of foodstuffs from minerals, and the growing of vast mountains of living meat in reservoirs of culture media, but something will have happened to the human species. If it survives under such conditions it will certainly survive only by beginning to turn into another kind of animal, and, from our point of view at least, not a very nice kind. We talk of the waning of the humanist tradition. It is specific humanness itself which is threatened. Montaigne or Sophocles could not flourish in present-day Jakarta. What are the beings that will be the fittest to survive when such communities have spread over the surface of the earth?

The probabilities are that man will discover ways to limit population during the next generation. Or perhaps the too probable nuclear war will solve the problem out of hand and reduce the population to a few millions in the Tropics and the Southern Hemisphere. Meanwhile, the inchoate spread of inhumane communities goes on. Urban renewal, what the French call *urbanisme,* suburbia, exurbia—aseptic slums proliferate.

We all remember the aquarium in our high-school biology

class, where the colony of volvox grew over in one corner, in the spot of optimum light and temperature. Man is altering, as it were, the temperature and light and salinity of his own aquarium, irrationally, and with no knowledge of the possible results. Nobody knows what may happen.

Nature makes man. Man makes culture. Culture makes man. Man destroys nature. Consider the ecologically stable environment out of which man as a species probably developed. It must have been something like the climax formation of the Eastern United States, a vast deciduous forest broken by parklands—only probably somewhat warmer. Where is that forest now? Does the present man-made environment of the Eastern United States bear any resemblance to it? How much of this kind of change can we stand? It is already greater than the ecological changes that set in in the late Jurassic and doomed the giant reptiles.

Archeologists and cultural anthropologists, and of course economists, often talk of culture as though it was just a mass of pots and arrowheads, ruined buildings, kinships, initiation ceremonies, food crops, value, price and profit—things and their relationships, sweeping inexorably through time, with no self-conscious chunks of human vitality around at all. Are we just vehicles for the evolution of our artifacts—which will eventually overwhelm and exterminate us?

This is the role of the architect, the landscape architect, the community planner—the creative reconstruction of our ecology. Today we have the knowledge and the techniques. It is perfectly possible to rebuild deliberately the human environment, in such a way that the ultimate result will be the widening and deepening of the life of the species as such, the augmenting increase of lifescope, esthetic enrichment in the most profound sense. This, I suppose, is the only kind of "creative evolution" of which we are capable. But it is possible that we are capable of that.

This is the purpose of a book such as Serge Chermayeff's *Community and Privacy: Toward a New Architecture of Humanism*. What he is talking about is much more than the efficient organization of the shelter of a community. At least his discussion is posited on an unusually profound sense of the meaning of the word "efficient." Le Corbusier was wrong, a house is *not* a machine for living in. The ideal community structure—the actual fabric of buildings and land—should be like a culture medium, like the optimum part of the tank where the Volvox flourished, a culture medium that stimulated and enriched, like a circumambient food, the creative responses of the community to its most human life.

We have a long tradition of community planning of this sort. We have a great deal of rather general or philosophical discussion. Geddes and Mumford are names known to every educated layman. But I know of few works that approach the problem so directly in terms of the actual physical structuring. What do we need for a biological optimum? How do we define these needs in terms of cubic feet of filled and empty spaces?

It would be easy to call Chermayeff's book a sort of exercise in human bio-technical engineering. It certainly is that, and masterfully so. It seems to me it is more than that. It is an exercise in creative or constructive humanism, but in a special sense. The guide here is such a work as Werner Jaeger's *Paideia*. We are to think in terms of a kind of higher hygiene—the planned ambience of the most abundant life.

What good will it all do? Can we possibly stop the avalanche of our own insensate constructions? I don't know. There are so many negative factors operating against the survival, let alone the evolution of the species, that the outlook is gloomy indeed. However, such books as Chermayeff's are a powerful force in the other direction. Who knows what single flicker of cosmic radiation once altered a gene somewhere back in geologic time and made all the difference? Certainly one book is a small but potent dose of creative evolution. Enough like it and the vast tides of our own biological history may, just may, turn.

1964

5.
Urbanism

When that I was but a little tiny lad there existed in America a fairly substantial organization devoted to realizing the city described in Edward Bellamy's *Looking Backward.** When I came to youth's estate I marvelled over the cities of the future, those illimitable geometrical icebergs that calved from the fertile Conté crayon of Norman Bel Geddes. In early manhood I was sold the radiant city of Le Corbusier because I had never seen an actual building by the man. Now the city of the future is here, and you can look at it in the pages of the picture magazines and the news weeklies. It looks just as pretty as it ever did in the pages of *Vanity Fair*. Living in it is another matter.

* This essay is based on a review of four books on urban renewal: Victor Gruen, *The Heart of Our Cities: The Urban Crisis: Diagnosis and Cure* (New York, Simon and Schuster, 1964); David R. Hunter, *The Slums: Challenge and Response* (Glencoe, Ill., The Free Press, 1964); Martin Anderson, *The Federal Bulldozer: A Critical Analysis of Urban Renewal, 1949–1962* (Cambridge, Mass., The M.I.T. Press, 1964); and Scott Greer, with the advice and assistance of Norton E. Long, *Metropolitics: A Study of Political Culture* (New York, John Wiley and Sons, 1964).

A recent lavish cover story in *Time* portrays the years of urban renewal as a spectacular success where squalor has been replaced by splendor to the satisfaction of all concerned. This is pure bunk. The first years of urban renewal were used simply to try to expel Negroes from potentially valuable property near the city centers. What resulted were acres of rubble punctuated by a few expensive, uncomfortable vertical ice-cube trays surrounded by a hard doughnut ring of doubled-up and redoubled slum dwellers. This, in cities where high-rise apartments and condominiums were already overbuilt. Across Thirty-Fifth Street from Lake Meadows, Chicago's Negro slums are doubling in density of population, which means that they are increasing geometrically in the social sicknesses known as "slum conditions." Northward the rubble stretches away where once stood the finest examples of America's finest domestic architecture—the work of Richardson and Sullivan and their contemporaries.

The pretty cover story describes San Francisco's urban renewal—called "Western Addition Number One"—as an accomplished fact. It is nothing of the sort. It is still mostly vacant lots, or as the French so appropriately call them, *terrains vagues*. Urban renewal, however, marches on to a new slum clearance, Western Addition Number Two, its slumification the result of the forced evacuation of Number One. So it goes across the country, except in some of the smaller communities where urban renewal has renewed the community practically out of existence—as witness a tragico-comical story in a recent *Nation* about a moribund small Texas town which died on the operating table.

Some of us who have been around a long time watching the rise and fall of modern architecture and its child or parent, urbanism, now realize that both are almost complete failures. A few young architects and planners too are beginning to revolt but the orthodox urban revolutionaries now have a mass audience, tax funds, and plenty of fellow travelers in the legislating bodies. Things are going to get worse before they get better.

There is little hint of this state of affairs in any of these books. David R. Hunter's *The Slums* may have been written for the great audience of self-informing laymen. It has more the character of supplementary reading for high-school seniors. It is not that it avoids controversy. Quite the contrary. Mr. Hunter presents "all sides" in such nicely non-partisan terms that they cancel each other out. If you had nothing else to go by you would believe that the slums and all their attendant ills were certain to come out clean and new from the laundromat of the democratic process. Alas, it's not true. Slums are essentially a frame of mind, a subjective state produced by economic and social forces which have little to do with architecture or city planning.

Up until two hundred years ago, every city in the world was all slum in the physical sense, with the possible exceptions of Venice and Hankow and, before them, Constantinople. The genuine urban revolutionaries are often accused by the planners of being archaistic and anti-city on principle. This is not true. A functioning city, a real *polis,* is a very good thing indeed. It is the optimum environment for the development of all the humane virtues. Humanism could well be defined as the way the inhabitants of a good city habitually behave. A good city is structured like an inclusion series. Built into it is an efficient hierarchy of social functions. If you have a society which is atomized, whose people have themselves no functional hierarchy but who are atomized and self-alienated, the places they live in are going to be slums no matter how much rent they pay or how much open space there is between the buildings. This has little to do with commercialism as such. The builders of Renaissance Florence—actually most of the city was completed in the Middle Ages—certainly built the buildings to make money. The builders of Magnitogorsk did not. Yet the first has not become a slum to this day while the second was born a slum. However, imagine what would happen to the old town of Florence if the present population were evacuated and replaced by the inhabitants of either Harlem or upper Fifth Avenue.

As far as the architecture and the planning are concerned, it is easily demonstrable that we are building worse slums than those we are tearing down, whether they are subsidized, low-rental housing or fantastically over-priced high-rise condominiums. The first, in fact, run a good chance of being better built than the second, especially in New York City, due to the stricter controls of Federal Housing. Outside the cities, of course, millions of acres of agricultural and recreational land have been destroyed by tract houses which will not outlast their amortization, and which are essentially congested even when they are on one-hundred-foot lots.

Victor Gruen, the author of *The Heart of Our Cities,* is in the business of correcting the City of the Future. There's nothing wrong with his plans but then there's nothing wrong with Plato's *Republic* or Kropotkin's *Fields, Factories and Workshops* either.

Gruen's basic ideas are traditional in the best sense. They go back to the founding fathers of urbanism. His central concept is a vision of the metropolis and its satellites structured in a hierarchy of organically interrelated facilities. This can be reduced to a schematic modulus which looks rather like the cross-section of a lower marine animal. Such an organism decorates the book jacket.

If Jane Jacob's book defending the old Faubourg communities of New York City was dismissed by the planners as sentimental and anachronistic, it nevertheless shook them up. Everybody admits now that we have to restore the neighborhood community. Mr. Gruen's plans in the last analysis add up to this. Each step towards the concentration of the center is a step from one functional community to another with a steady increase of scope and intensity of public demand. This is the basis of city planning. What does it mean?

The outer ring of the city would consist of residences, shops, and services for daily use; the next ring, multiple dwellings with the same essential services, larger shops, and occasional services, for instance, doctors. The center of the city would consist of long-term services, banks, brokerages, hospitals, and high-rise apartments and the largest stores, closed to automobile traffic and set amidst parks and promenades. Here too would be concentrated the major cultural activities of the entire city. Factories and other mass employers of labor would be confined to the outskirts and would communicate with each other and with the residential areas by encircling freeways and by a limited number which would cross the city and divide it into semi-self-sufficient segments.

This in fact is a schematic picture of the way most cities are structured at present. The difference between Victor Gruen's modulus and reality is a difference of efficiency. If a city were rationally planned or reorganized in terms of its inherent functional patterns, it would presumably not only be more orderly but more beautiful—a wholesome environment of the civic virtues.

There is nothing wrong with this, but who is going to bell the cat? Just one example out of many—the automobile is obsolete. Everything about it is obsolete. The internal combustion engine, the drive line, the control mechanism, the fuel, the sales organization, and the production methods with their attendant labor structure. Of course it is destroying the cities of the world—Paris, Florence, London have become unlivable. As Frank Lloyd Wright said, it is easier to get someplace in New York crawling over the tops of the taxicabs than inside one. Los Angeles is an illimitable rose-covered slum gashed with freeways, all its potential foci of community long since devoured by parking lots, its population dying of *anomie* under a mile-high blanket of carcinogens.

As Katharine Mansfield said when she read James Joyce's *Ulysses,* "This is the future and I'm glad I've got tuberculosis." What can Mr. Gruen point to? A few pedestrian malls on former Main Streets. His favorite is Rochester, which looks a little brassy to me and which certainly cannot solve alone the urban diseases which afflict that city. Better still is the adoption in a simplified and improved form of his own rejected spectacular Forth Worth plan by the city of Fresno, California. So far this has worked out very well indeed. The pedestrian mall is a tremendous success commercially as well as socially and most of the city is enthusiastic for the further development of the plan. Fort Worth, alas, had lost the chance to become one of the handsomest and most efficient cities in the world. There the Gruen plan was defeated by a united front of parking-lot interests. It is this class of small-minded, large-scale but still petty bourgeois business interests which, with the real-estate operators, makes up the irreducible opposition to any kind of civilized urban planning whatsoever.

I think Gruen believes that we are at a technological tipover point where private enterprise can once again make money out of urban and interurban rapid transit. I hope so, but I see little evidence of it. Suburban trains and city autobuses lose money now running on four wheels. I don't think they'll suddenly become profitable if you just take off two wheels and turn them into monorails. People have been talking about moving sidewalks since Bellamy and H. G. Wells, but free enterprise has never shown any inclination to build one of any length.

Whatever its faults and they are largely those of optimism, Victor Gruen's book is by far the most stimulating and illuminating treatment of the subject to be published in many years, and unlike many of the early epochal works, like Le Corbusier's, it is written by a man who knows what he is talking about, a man in the business of redesigning cities with a vast experience in all the human, economic, and political problems involved in the struggle to achieve an operable human ecology.

The Federal Bulldozer is a point-by-point devastating criticism of Federal urban renewal. In fact it is so devastating that it is hard to believe, but I have yet to see a convincing denial of any of its charges. However, its conclusion that private enterprise can do better is most dubious. If it can why hasn't it? A very large proportion of the population of our cities is spending 25 per cent or more of income on housing. What would have happened to the class of birds if at some time in its evolutionary history all birds would have had to spend a quarter of their time every day in the year building their nests? Urban renewal under the pressure of the civil-rights organizations is being forced to undertake more and more subsidized housing. That may not be much of a gain but it's better than nothing.

Scott Greer's *Metropolitics* is the story of efforts to restructure the metropolitan areas of St. Louis, Miami, and Cleveland. It is a scientifically objective study with all sorts of apparatus and "discipline" which is really concerned with subjects which in a ruder day Lincoln Steffens handled more discursively and subjectively. It would not be properly scientific and value neuter today to call a book *The Shame of the Cities*.

Behind the charts and statistics moves a sad, sad comedy of ignorance and covetousness. In all questions of urbanism the enemy is not in the "bastions of entrenched greed" but in thousands of foxholes and pillboxes of stupidity and selfishness, and of course behind the scenes in all the battles of American urban affairs there move almost invisible, like the political commissars through the trenches of a Bolshevik Army—plain, ordinary criminals. What is wrong with American civic life is not the magnificos at the glittering pinnacle of the power structure. It is the great middle class, small business, petty executives, and crooked politicians, those people with the well-shined shoes whose activities make up what the rest of the world calls the American way of life—and the Mafia.

Scott Greer's concluding sentence might well end any book ever written on urbanism: "The efforts to make the Heavenly City may be compared to fish eggs, spawned by the million, lost and devoured by other organisms, but occasionally producing a new model which could not have been predicted or designed but may have virtues of its own."

Nobody likes to face the fact that an ever-increasing percentage—long since the majority—of the population prefers to live in slums. Few apartments ever built are structurally anything else. Adequate baths, separate kitchens and dining rooms, separate baths and water closets, even separate sleeping rooms, high ceilings and even large rooms as such are actively disliked by most of the customers for real estate. Apartment houses which discard all of the amenities are very successful financially even in the bedroom suburbs. On the other hand, new or remodeled town houses where they have been adventured as part of urban renewal have proved very difficult to sell.

There are a number of "neo-Victorian" townhouse projects going up around the country but their sale seems to be limited almost exclusively to mildly eccentric and exceptionally affluent intellectuals, while warrens of massive gimcrackery take over the best sites in Greenwich Village. This does not reflect just the vulgarity and rapacity of the real-estate operators; it reflects conscious choice. People who demand good homes, in either single or multiple form, can find developers who will provide them. Where most Americans prefer to live, only Roman slaves were domiciled in any previous time and they were there presumably against their wishes.

There is another aspect of this problem which is never mentioned. Perhaps we have already passed a point of no return and the problems now confronting people in their attempts to live together can never be solved with the solutions we want. The Malthusian problem may not be an economic one at all. A Jesuit demographer has proven conclusively to his own satisfaction that the earth can support eleven billion people. The crux is the definition of the word "people." Perhaps the Malthusian problem is an ecological one, or, if you will, an esthetic one. There may be a point, and a rather low one, at which our species, as we know it, can be said to have saturated both the earth's surface and its local environment. Beyond that point it will start turning into something else, something that we, as humane humans, would find very disagreeable. Maybe that point has been passed and nothing now can reverse the process.

Chicago has the finest promenade in America, Michigan Boulevard. Not only was it the home of what may well be the greatest domestic architects who ever lived, but most of the city for an eight-mile radius from the civic center was built by contractors under very strict building codes and in sound imitation of the work of those great master architects. It has had an urban general plan all this century unequalled in the nobility of its conception. Most of that plan has long since been realized. The city is a network of parks and boulevards and playgrounds. It is surrounded by a greenbelt recreational forest preserve. For thirty miles it faces on a beautiful lake lined with parks and beaches. From Evanston to the Indiana line and indefinitely west into the hinterland it is all one intolerable slum from which people escape if they can, or endure in truculent misery if they cannot. The best thing to do with Chicago would be to walk away and leave it to the archeologists of the year 5000. But where to? Los Angeles? Leopoldville? Irkutsk? Jakarta? Manhattan?

Note: In 1964 the "New York Review of Books" which had commissioned this piece asked me to rewrite it, as it was "too provincial." I never rewrite for any *editor.*

6.
Poetry in 1965

American poetry, like most artistic activity every place, comes by fits and starts. The Imagists, "Others," the Lost Generation, the Proletarians, the Reactionaries, the Trotskyites, the Beats—in between lie periods of quiescence when the geyser is grumbling underground and gathering its strength. The brief periods when the geyser is blowing off, and poetry is hot copy, have not necessarily been the times of greatest creativity.

The Imagist movement produced only a couple of poets of importance. In fact, many critics consider H. D. the only Imagist. The Proletarians, alas, produced none. At the height of their notoriety there were never more than two Beat poets, Ginsberg and Corso. The only important group to constitute a movement, as such things are seen by the press, was the generation of Classic Modernists—William Carlos Williams, Wallace Stevens, Marianne Moore, Mina Loy, Walter Conrad Arensberg, Maxwell Bodenheim—and so on for some thirty names, who were published by Alfred Kreymborg in his magazine and yearbook, *Others,* 1916-1919, and even the majority of them have been forgotten. Between commotions, which is most of the time, American poetry trundles along quietly on a plateau. The last seven or eight years have been such a period.

There have been no sensations. Plenty of poetry has been written, which in another time would have been shocking enough, but it has met with critical indifference. Our reflexes tired early in the PR racket raised by the Beats. Nobody really cares if you manage to write a poem using more dirty words per page than Allen Ginsberg. The New Village on the Lower East Side pullulates with coffee shops and mimeographs where barefoot boys and girls defy the Post Office, but the Post Office has smartened up and has refused to defy back.

We have evolved surefire formulas for alienation. We not only have a rigorously organized academy of outcasts with uniforms and passwords, but the outcasts have entered the most respectable academies. Most of the Black Mountain group, including Robert Creeley and Charles Olson, are now professors just like everybody else, and busy teaching the daughters of small-town used-car dealers in colleges in the Bible Belt, the piney woods, and the wheatlands, how to make like Van Gogh, Rimbaud, and Artaud in one semester one hour a week, and get two and one half credits for doing it.

Meanwhile, the old official Academia—the organization led by John Crowe Ransom and Allen Tate—trundles along in its own peculiar trough, turning out little reactionaries, all as alike as the faces on a sheet of stamps. I suppose that the most significant development of the last few years is that the Reactionary Generation has at last become totally infertile. No real poets of this kidney have come up in the last ten years. The poetic school of Thomas Nelson Page has run dry at last.

Instead of the literary Alexandrianism and political obscurantism characteristic of American academic verse for so many years, today most English departments seem to have accepted their limitations. They turn out what might be called "white-collar verse." Presumably, as automation renders even the engineers redundant, the qualifications for bureaucrats and technocrats in the last quarter of the twentieth century will include the ability to write harmlessly complicated domestic verse, its ambiguities carefully calculated by slide rule. Already the output is illimitable.

A surprising number of publishers now issue paperbacks of contemporary verse. University presses like Wesleyan and Indiana apparently consider them prestige items. Where once there was only the Yale Series of Younger Poets, there are now ten or more such series.

I am all for it, but I think it the better part of valor to understand what it is. If the English departments can provide the typical young smalltown auto dealer, IBM branch manager, or CPA with a set of literary counters that he can rearrange on the page when he takes the kids for a hike by the reservoir, when he falls in love, or when his mother dies, it seems to me this is all to the good. High civilization has always been based on a broad foundation of cultivated bureaucrats. I don't understand why my friends who teach creative writing to future bureaucrats are so infuriated when I say this.

Literally speaking, Series of Younger Poets and Poetry Awards are the kiss of death. The oldest, the Yale effort, has always been governed by the highest motives, and its present and its penultimate editors, W. H. Auden and Dudley Fitts, I consider friends and gentlemen of discretion. Looking back over the record, however, is a queasy experience. Once in a while, by some mysterious accident, a poet sneaked in—Stephen Vincent Benét or Muriel Rukeyser—but who were all those other people? The present editor has obviously tried to break away from this tradition of worse-than-mediocrity. In recent years a couple of his choices, notably Jack Gilbert, have been good indeed. The point that I am making is, that even with the best intentions and the most imaginative editors, there is something wrong. This is not the way that significant poetry usually gets published, and when it does it is all too obviously an accident.

It is almost impossible to keep track, much less to read through, all the verse now being published. If you do sit down and try to, the steady diet of mediocrity so dulls your responses that, when something good does come along, you are likely to miss it. Therefore, before I started to write this piece I polled my friends. I wrote a dozen poets of unquestioned ability and of the most disparate tastes—"Would you be so kind as to return the enclosed post card with the names of three poets under thirty-five you consider the best?" Everybody voted, but most of the people preferred to remain anonymous. Allen Ginsberg sent me three letters, each with about ten people on it. One person wrote on his card, "There are no good poets under thirty-five."

The names that occurred most often were Gary Snyder, Tim Reynolds, Arienne Rich, Thom Gunn. It's a curious thing that several of my correspondents seemed to have overlooked their own increasing years, and named people now well past thirty-five. As a matter of fact, I think this may be true of two of the people who got the most votes. Gary Snyder and Tim Reynolds were popular with representatives of all tastes except the most Beat. Otherwise the choices tend to represent definite schools.

Here's the list: A. R. Ammons, Robert Bly, Michael Benedikt, Wendell Berry, Diane di Prima, Edward Dorn, Richard Duerdon, William Duffy, Russell Edson, Harry Fainlight, Jack Gilbert, Ronald Johnson, LeRoi Jones, Robert Kelly, William Knott, Ron Loewinsohn, Lewis Lipsitz, Jay Macpherson, Michael McClure, Daniel Moore, Richard Moore, Jim Mosley, David Ray, Jerome Rothenberg, Ed Sanders, James Scully, Anne Sexton, Dick Shaw, Susan Sherman, Joel Sloman, Gil Sorrentino, A. B. Spellman, Philip Whalen, John Wieners, Miller Williams, Jonathan Williams.

I have listed everybody's choices except Allen Ginsberg's. His letters were practically a history of postwar bohemia, so I had to make my own choice of poets from his list. Robert Bly said in his letter, "I don't see any pattern in these, and very little that they have in common unless it were much more dependence on naked imagination than the poets—who put their confidence more in form and 'structure'—preceding them. I think that's a good thing."

I think he is right about the total list but I also think that this, in itself, is a definite and significant pattern. Robert Bly, James Wright, and their associates on *The Sixties;* Cid Corman (the most dedicated man in American literature) in his magazine, *Origin;* John Logan with his handsome new magazine, *Choice;* a small group of young Catholic poets who publish in the Catholic magazines, *Critic, Jubilee, Ramparts* and *Commonweal,* as well as in *The Sixties* and *Choice;* and the constantly changing publications of the East Village coffee shops, and their like numbers in San Francisco's North Beach—they all have one thing in common. They no longer find it necessary to be in revolt against the formalist tradition and its exclusive echoing of the stylistic exercises of the textbook poets of English—that is, British—literature. Hard, slogging work by the Reactionary Generation, in the years just before and during World War II, managed to cut American poetry completely free from the international literature of the twentieth century and return it to a position of provincial dependence it enjoyed before Longfellow translated Provençal and imitated the *Kalevala.* Now we have returned.

Three principles have guided all the editors of poetry magazines of the last ten years. One: anti-formalism; the chances of a baroque sonnet packed with seventy-seven euphemistic ambiguities being printed today, except in the quarterlies of the Old Guard—the *Partisan, Kenyon,* and *Hudson* reviews—are remote indeed.

Two: re-internationalization. Robert Bly, especially, has published a great deal of foreign poetry in *The Sixties;* poets like Yves Bonnefoy and Alain Bosquet have enjoyed considerable social and platform success in America, although the most significant French poet ever to live in this country, Claude Vigée, came and went in the decade after the war unrecognized by the American poets in the very colleges where he taught French literature, and utterly unknown to the American poet who most resembled him, Delmore Schwartz. A situation like this would be highly unlikely ever to happen again. We are ecumenical again, as we were from 1912 to 1929.

Three: directness of statement, objectivism, presentational immediacy. It is difficult to think of a term which covers the whole range of the re-affirmation of the anti-literary, no-nonsense esthetic of the days of Imagism and literary cubism, as well, of course, as of literary Populism. Carl Sandburg, H. D.,

Gertrude Stein, shared a repugnance towards literary cookery. This attitude, transmitted to the young largely through the work of William Carlos Williams and the re-discovered Louis Zukofsky, is shared by almost all the poets of this generation, however else they may disagree or how utterly antagonistic they may be in personality, from Anne Sexton to Ed Sanders, the Superbeat who puts out a mimeographed unprintable magazine.

Thus, the group of young Catholic poets shares neither the politics nor the esthetics of the *Criterion's* garbled importations from *L'Action française* nor T. S. Eliot's nor Donald Davidson's provincial popularizations of the principles of Léon Daudet, Massis, and Maurras; in other words, they are not neo-Catholics, but just plain Catholics. This change is a more important symptom than one might imagine. It represents, in one specifically delimited area of American culture, the return of a provincial literature to the literature of the contemporary world.

Beatniks, teddy boys, Mods and Rockers, *stilyagi* are obviously an international movement. In the period of imminent nuclear extinction, McCarthyism, and the Zhdhanovtchina, the international power structure was given over to seemingly unbridled nihilism and found a reflection of its nihilism at the bottom of society amongst the voluntary outcasts, just as the irresponsible nihilistic tyranny of the czars produced the historic Nihilists. Of course, we are not out of the woods yet, and so the literature of violent alienation not only still exists, but has become extremely popular amongst the young.

It is significant, though, that beards and bare feet, leotards and free-verse doggerel full of dirty words, are now on their second time around. A few years back, if you showed up on the campus of a sophisticated university in holey tennis shoes and torn blue jeans, people would say, "Did you just get sprung from the ice cream parlor by Oshkosh high school?" Today they are back in droves, but it is significant that they all wear nuclear disarmament buttons and spend a good deal of their time sitting in, lying in, going limp, and sleeping in. Ten years ago, when the little toy dog was new and *On the Road* and *Howl* were still in manuscript, the slogan (to quote the madman in the Bandhouse described by Nelson Algren in *Never*

Come Morning) was "Let them horses gallop, let them snakes wiggle, let them camels hump, LET EVERYTHING GO!"

Today, it's an up-to-date version of the banners of my youth —FREE LOVE, FREE LIQUOR, FREE MOONEY. It is no longer alienation but revolt. However revolting its conduct, revolt it still is. The very notion of the faintest hint of social responsibility would fill the souls of the elder statesmen of the beatniks with disgust. Ed Sanders' mimeographed sheet resembles an occupational-therapy project in a very permissive asylum, but his people are genuinely concerned about the evils of society—war, sexual conflict and racial persecution, commercialism, and literary hypocrisy. The fact that they can't get beyond free-verse doggerel full of dirty words may leave them impoverished as writers, but it only cripples, it does not invalidate, their posture of social responsibility. Once they moved on to become The Fugs, Sanders and especially Tuli Kupferberg discovered their most effective weapon, humor. Only the aging and the fools in this group, for instance, persist in glorifying the Negro for his disabilities. They no longer worship him because they think he takes dope. Since he was discovered by Jack Kerouac, an appreciable number of the young literateurs of the East Side Village have actually met a Negro. Again, this may seem to be an unimportant group; their mimeographed publications are unknown to the great public; their coffeeshop readings never seat more than fifty people; the man on the street never heard of them, even though an appreciable number of Harlem and Village streetwalkers have. The self-proclaimed youth of Western and laterally Eastern and African society has been characterized by, to echo Thorstein Veblen's phrase, "conspicuous expenditure" of spirit. The commotion seems childish, produces remarkably few real artists, but the social effect of the militant *jeunesse* is insidious and slow maturing. They grow older. They do not become professional poets or painters—on the contrary, they give up bohemia, *la vie scandaleuse,* get jobs and acquire families, and the day comes when some of them are ambassadors, bank presidents, and chainstore managers. Vestigial remnants of their adolescent ideologies survive to become the accepted mores of their middle age. Today, as is well known, the top floors on

Madison Avenue would be drastically thinned of executive talent if they suddenly lost all alumni of the John Reed Club, the Red writers' and artists' organization of 1932.

Robert Creeley and Charles Olson, formerly of the *Black Mountain Review,* have become inactive as editors. To a certain extent, their place has been taken by Jonathan Williams, editor of *Jargon,* and Denise Levertov, now Poetry Editor of the *Nation,* who publishes the young poets who form a kind of second generation of the Black Mountain group, for instance, Gil Sorrentino, Susan Sherman, John Weiners, and Robert Kelly. I suppose they could be best characterized as sharing objective imagery, a kind of shameless pathos and ironic wit. This description, of course, could apply equally well to their immediate ancestor, Robert Creeley, or even to Denise.

The better academic poets, of whom Thom Gunn, Adrienne Rich, and Tim Reynolds are fitting examples, like their immediate predecessors, do not write baroque metaphysical verse derived from the theories of William Empson and John Crowe Ransom. They are moved by a quite contrary esthetic—they are neo-classical or simplistic. Their models are Hardy and Landor, rather than Donne and Chapman; their mentor, if any, is Yvor Winters. However, the baroque tradition of metaphysical conceit, artificial emotionalism, complex structure and lush ornamentation dies hard. The poets whom Robert Bly says "depend more on naked imagination" might well accuse Tim Reynolds, a poet of very great promise, of still suffering from excessive cookery. It is difficult for him, as it is for Adrienne Rich, to escape from the long-established kitchen of ambiguity and artifice—which is doubtless why they are most popular with the older generation.

I think the most significant group of young poets are those published in *Choice* and *The Sixties,* and the most significant of these is certainly William Knott, who writes under the whimsical pseudonym of Saint Geraud. Saint Geraud, in case you don't know, was a nasty monk, the hero of a pornographic classic. Knott's poems are remarkable for their chasteness. In fact, that might be said to be their distinguishing characteristic. Even when they are about sleeping together, they impart an emotion of great purity which can only be called connubial bliss. There are a few things like this in modern literature, perhaps Yvon and Claire Goll's *Ten Thousand Dawns—Dix Mille Aubes*—the very title of which has always brought tears to my eyes. It is significant that the comparison that should spring to mind is a European one, and that of a couple who wrote fluently in English, French, and German. If Robert Bly has fulfilled no other plank of his program, he has certainly encouraged mighty steps on the part of young poets towards a return to the international community.

Richard Shaw, Jerome Rothenberg, David Ray, Michael Benedikt, William Duffy, Russell Edson might just as well be writing in French or Polish, yet they are intensely autochthonous. Mark that they share this characteristic with absolute aboriginals like William Carlos Williams. It has always been true that it is our localists who are universal and our imitators of latest Bloomsbury fads who are hopelessly provincial. Mr. Eliot has never been able to escape from that lilac-filled backyard in St. Louis, while literate Uzbeks have learned from Dr. Williams the exact perfume of the fetor of the Jersey mudflats.

A generation ago when Yeats, in his preface, dismissed Wilfred Owen with the observation "the poetry was" most emphatically *not* "in the pity," he scandalized everybody. I'm afraid he was right, and nothing bears him out more than most contemporary Negro poetry. The relation between the races in America is in fact a tragedy or a mortal sin, but artistically, it is a bore. It is a shocking state of affairs, but it doesn't make for art. Race poetry, "protest poetry," self-evidently can say nothing new. Alas, white editors want little else. If you're colored and enclose a photograph, you can publish almost anything, as long as it's about dope, saxophones, lynchings, urine-stained hallways, and murderous miscegenation. The most militant Negro poets of the youngest generation are precisely those who resist the demands of this factitious market. Most of LeRoi Jones' best poetry ignores race, except implicitly, and even where he does use it, as in certain bitterly sarcastic erotic poems, nothing is really lost to the poem if you cross out or exchange the words "black" and "white." LeRoi Jones is certainly the best, as he is the most influential of widely published young Negro poets. There may be plenty of others, but it is impossible to tell, because editors print only their race poetry.

The best recent anthology is *Beyond the Blues,* published in England by The Hand and Flower Press, and edited by Rosey E. Pool, who is a Dutchwoman. Here again, the young poets who make the most impact are those who avoid explicit racial protest. Typical of the best is Julia Field, whose poetry has poignancy that might be the expression of any race. She and the few others like her might be said to represent the arrival of *negritude* in American verse, that is, she has pride in her race, because she had pride in herself. I think that this question is a most important crux of esthetic judgment—it points up the most basic of all issues. It is a moral problem, essentially but it is directly reflected in artistic structure.

E. N. Sargent's *The African Boy* is a deliberate, self-conscious effort at *negritude* in Sedar-Senghor's exact sense, that is, "the sum total of the values which characterize black civilization." It even sounds like him, or Diop, or Niger, or Césaire. You could expect this to invalidate it or, at least, reduce it to the level of the anthropological ballet once so popular and so unbelievable. On the contrary it's surprisingly convincing, but not as the few young Negro poets who do not need to be deliberate about their *negritude.* It is by a white woman.

The last ten years have seen a great burst of poetic activity amongst young Catholic writers. Doubtless, this is another symptom of what a caustic Cardinal called "the end of Pius IX's war with the nineteenth century" or another ecclesiastic, the "tentative return of the Church to the human race." It is curious, however, that these young intellectuals lag far behind their own hierarchy—and the American hierarchy is far from being the most revolutionary element in the Church. Most of the young Catholic poets write ingenuous lyrics to which faint echoes of the liturgy lend a slight flavor of exoticism. There is no hint yet in America of the passionate drive towards social responsibility and ethical activism which distinguishes the young men of the French Catholic Left. In America we only have *The Catholic Worker,* which is ingenuous to a fault, and J. F.

Powers, who does not write poetry. (This has changed in five years.)

Finally, Cid Corman, since we are talking about religion, could certainly be called a literary saint. Ever since the war he has lived a life of the strictest voluntary poverty and has saved most of a tiny income from the G.I. Bill or from small fellowships and used it to publish *Origin,* a magazine which he gives away free to anyone who asks for it. He not only publishes all the significant young poets but he has also conscientiously reflected their revaluation of the past. He has, for instance, given more space to the Objectivist poet of the Twenties, Louis Zukofsky, than any three magazines in the past forty years. Like Robert Bly, he has also published translations from a variety of languages which reflect precisely contemporary taste.

One of Corman's favorites is Gary Snyder, the poet who got the largest number of votes from my colleagues. I think he deserved them. He is a Protean young man with a vast range of solid knowledge and has already accumulated years of experience in real, as distinguished from literary and academic life. That is, he is a Buddhologist, learned in Sanskrit, Pali, Chinese, and Japanese—as far from a Zen Beatnik as might be; he lived for a long time inside a Japanese monastery, not out in the garden with the Chicago millionairesses; at Reed College, where he was a four-year sensation, a sensation that endures to this day, he was a major in anthropology; he has done all the things young Pacific roustabouts do for a living—worked in the woods, on the sea and on the docks, picked fruit and worked with horses and cows. This is what distinguishes Gary Snyder. He has a lot to say and an urgent need to say it, and he is, of all these people, most the master of a complex and mature style.

There are a number of poets who are not easy to categorize, and elude any schematic presentation of contemporary verse. Jack Gilbert will have to stand for all of them. Easy technical skill, sharply ironic wit—I suppose it is his maturity which enables him to elude categorization and I suppose that it is one of definition of maturity.

Perhaps it is best to sum up on that note. With the exception of the neo and post-Beats of the unprintable school, who are incorrigibly bare-bottomed boys with cheeks of tan, the last five years of American poetry give the impression of being a little more at ease, a little more at home in the wide world of literature, and even life, than their predecessors. They are quieter; their blood runs thinner, but they are a step nearer to being men of letters. It seems to me that that must be counted a gain because everybody knows that it's men of letters we need in America and surely don't have.

1965

7.

Why Is American Poetry Culturally Deprived?

André Malraux is famous for the remark that American literature is the only contemporary literature not written by intellectuals. He points out that general ideas of any subtlety or profundity are unknown to all major American novelists, poets, and dramatists. Partly of course this judgment was motivated by Malraux's own taste. The only writers acceptable to him are Faulkner, Hemingway, Tennessee Williams, Raymond Chandler, Dashiell Hammett, the militantly mindless. In fact, shortly after the war, both Malraux and Roger Caillois happened to have said to me that they considered somebody named "Orass Mikwa" America's most significant writer. It was some time before I figured out that this was the semi-literate pulp magazine writer of the blood-on-the-bikini school, Horace McCoy.

Nevertheless, Malraux's judgment is substantially correct. I have known the leading exponents of all the movements in American poetry which presumed ideological motivation, that at least attempted to assume the language of those general ideas which were part of the storm and stress of international thought. Without exception, these ideas came to their poet exponents only through the most superficial literary journalism, were never comprehended, either the simple elements or their consequences, and were never in fact acted upon. Let me detail this. Carl Sandburg could stand as an example of the Social Democratic and Populist writers of 1910, a colleague of Richard Dehmel and Émile Verhaeren and Romain Rolland. Sandburg is usually considered to have bankrupted himself as an artist by betraying these ideas when America entered the First War. The fact is he didn't have any ideas to betray. His attitude towards "the people" was a compound of Chicago police-court reporter sentimentality, Midwest smalltown Populist oratory, and Hull House maidenly magnanimity. The picture of the young Sandburg breathlessly following the debates in the international Socialist movement over Bernstein's Revisionism, the Millerand crisis, Luxemburg and Kautsky disputing the questions of imperialism and the falling rate of profit is so ridiculous it is not even laughable.

The Modernist movement in verse, from the Imagists to the old masters of modern verse, first extensively published in Alfred Kreymborg's *Others,* the period of *Broom* and *The Little Review,* was a movement of technical reform of syntax and a cleaning up of the vocabulary of poetry. It has often been compared to the Symbolist movement in France. None of these poets, with the exception of Amy Lowell, John Gould Fletcher, Walter Conrad Arensberg, Ezra Pound, Wallace Stevens, William Carlos Williams, and T. S. Eliot, read European poetry or knew anything about it. In their French classes in college the last poet in the course had been Jules Laforgue. Therefore, insofar as they paid attention to their lessons, he represented for them the last word in French modernism. He died in 1887. He still represents the last word in French modernism for American academic versifiers. The profound revolutions of the sensibility, the climactic changes in the soul of modern man, so-called, which began with Baudelaire, Kierkegaard, Newman, Dostoievsky, and Nietzsche and which represent in fact a systematic destructive criticism of the foundations of humanism and humanitarianism, and which have thrown up in the course of their ever-accelerating liquidation all the anti-humane art movements and philosophies of our time, were, to judge from the evidence, totally incomprehensible to the American imitators of their stylistic innovations—even at the remove of fifty years. It should never be forgotten that H. D. was a contemporary of the Dadaists. French and German literature was falling to pieces with heartbreak. The veriest schoolboy in Europe, as Lord Macaulay used to say, knew that civilization had betrayed itself. H. D. was dedicating herself to cleaning and brightening the idiom of the Sapphic poets, Michael Field and Renée Vivien. Over against such much abused esthetes there was only Midwest Populism, whose intellectual foundations never rose higher than an editorial in a Des Moines newspaper. Out of the ranks of what were to become the Classic Modernists, two young men from the remote hinterland rose in revolt, T. S. Eliot and Ezra Pound. Pound most emphatically was not a member of the international community of letters, any more than any other emigré café sitter, then or now. Drinking Pernod on the sidewalk of the Dôme then, or the Flore now, never made Pound a cubist nor has it, if you will forgive the French word, made any "foundation bum" an *existentialiste*. Pound was under the impression that his café companions, Max Elskamp and Georges Fourrest, were the leaders of French poetry. This, at the height of the careers of Reverdy, Éluard, Aragon, with Apollinaire only dead a year. Eliot, on the other hand, did attach himself to an international community—the movement of virulent obscurantism and clerical fascism led by Henri Massis and Maurras and given voice in *L'Action française*. It should not be forgotten that the real reason for the international failure of this movement was that it was so reactionary that practical politicians like Hitler and Mussolini found it unusable. When *L'Action française* said, "We are not interested in the opinions of an obscure Jewish carpenter who met a disgraceful death two thousand years ago, but in restoring to France the order and glory [*gloire*—a bit of French slang recently restored to currency] of Richelieu and Mazarin," the Holy Office excommunicated them by telegram. This is not an idle, an unsubstantiated accusation against Mr. Eliot. He is not only on record as being an anti-Semite, but on record as being in favor of eliminating the Jews, and a surprising number of the French contributors to *The Criterion* ended up in the dock as war criminals.

Now, it so happens that if any international community recruited English and American poets in the interbellum period, it was fascism—Pound, Yeats, Eliot are on record. This is not because American poets are exceptionally vicious men, although some of them are and have been. It is simply because fascism is so much more easily assimilated by simple and emotionally unstable minds—you don't have to read so many books. As the economic depression deepened and their betters began talking about economics, most of this generation of American poets became money cranks, followers of the Social Credit theories of Major Douglas. This is an ancient American foolishness. I don't doubt for a moment but what as the fur market moved inexorably westward to Michillimakinac, the Grand Sachems of the Iroquois believed they could call it back by fooling with the wampum. Funny-moneyism is precisely a symptom of the incorrigible provinciality of small-town debtors in the American Outback. When the actual levers of power are so remote as to be unimaginable, their victims always resort to sympathetic magic. Although Mr. Eliot is reputed to have worked in a bank, it didn't help. No one used to handling general ideas, no one familiar with elementary facts of, to use a sound but old-fashioned term, political economy, as those facts and general ideas work themselves out in the real affairs of men, would ever fall for such flimsy nonsense as Major Douglas's Social Credit.

Like a faint chorus of young birds in the nests, echoes of Mr. Eliot's principled reaction suddenly were heard amongst the moonshine of the Southern Hills. Mr. Ransom, Mr. Tate, and their friends at Vanderbilt, meeting in the parlor of a Greek letter fraternity, launched the frail vessel of American reaction. Alas, the cargo was too slight for even so puny a ship. Mr. Eliot's *The Criterion,* carried on its manifest bales of Massis, Maurras, and Maritain, as reinterpreted by Fernandez, Saurez, and Bernard Fay, and Pareto and Major Douglas reinterpreted by Ezra Pound and Wyndham Lewis, and the Almighty as reinterpreted by the followers of Gurdjieff. Mr. Tate, and Mr. Ransom, could manage no more than the ideological residues of *Red Rock* and *The Clansman*. True, there was vague echo of the Physiocrats but an echo bounced off the surface of the thinker of the Fugitives' new agrarian group, a professor who seems to have been a ghost writer for a number of leading Southern personalities from Governor Long and Senator Bilbo to Governor Wallace. This is as near as serious thought amongst American poets ever came to the international discussions which raged throughout the interbellum period about the role of the élite, the threats of mass culture, the relations of town and country.

Many of these people were connected with the absurd Humanist movement of the pre-crisis Twenties. Today it is obvious that this was just a power drive on the part of a number of young academicians to recapture book-reviewing jobs from the Populist disciples of H. L. Mencken, who threatened to monopolize them. It was successful, but unimportant in the arena of world thought.

Throughout the period of proletarian literature, I never knew a Communist poet who was able to read through the first, much less the third volume of *Capital*. It was looked upon as a dry, dull, exclusively technical book. Of course, what's wrong with it is its highly emotional rhetoric and its elementary sleight-of-hand mathematics. God knows, it's absorbing enough reading, as absorbing as the Isaiah to which it has often been compared, but the Marxists of the Thirties judged Marx as the contributors to *Commentary* of the Fifties judged Isaiah—dry, dull, excessively technical. American poets just don't read non-fiction.

Since the Second War the literary quarterlies which started out under an alliance of Southern reactionaries and ex-Trotskyites have, it is true, tried to give their readers some inkling of some of the intellectual currents in the maëlstrom of post-war European thought. This has meant, pretty much, Existentialism, but with the exception of Lionel Abel, no poet has contributed to this discussion. What is more significant, not a single autochthonous idea has come up in the literary quarterlies of the post-war period. We live in a time of continuous revaluation. It is a time when it seems less and less possible to do anything overtly and therefore a time given over to relentless subjective subversion. There is no sign of this revaluation in America—our think pieces in our leading intellectual quarterlies never rise above the *ABC of Zen Buddhism, What Is Existentialism, How to Appreciate the Theatre of the Absurd in Easy Lessons for Small-Town Clergymen, Over-read Clubwomen, and Candidates for Ph.D.'s.* Modern thought is haunted by a sense of crisis. We live in an eschatological age. This sense of crisis is not new. It began in the 1840's. But for the past two generations, there has solidified a tradition of crisis-thinking which is now almost universal, a true universe of discourse from which no one seems to be able to escape. Niccolo Hartmann, Scheler, Berdyaev, Buber, Tillich, Marcel, Mounier—these men are in fact anti-Existentialist, but even they are swept up in the general mass movement of anguish and anxiety, I have never met an American poet who was familiar with Jean-Paul Sartre's attempts at philosophy, much less with the gnarled discourse of Scheler or Heidegger.

This is not quite true. Lionel Abel is an exception. He even went to Paris and met Jean-Paul Sartre personally, and for a year could be seen on the Boulevard St. Germain eavesdropping on his conversations with Simone de Beauvoir and Jean Wahl. There's only one trouble. Although he is a pretty good playwright, Lionel Abel is not a major poet. The same is true of Paul Goodman, who not only is part of the discourse of modern international thought, but who has certainly tried hard all his life to be an honestly original thinker. Again, he's not one of our most important poets. Similarly, in the Marxist epoch, John Brooks Wheelwright not only knew more about Marx than Earl Browder, he knew very much more about St. Thomas Aquinas than T. S. Eliot and Mortimer Adler rolled together. All three of these people, Goodman, Abel, Wheelwright—and the forgotten poet disciple of Wittgenstein, Lou Grudin—would be immensely important figures if they had written in French or even German or Italian. For over a generation, they have been the think tanks from which the editors of *The Partisan Review* drew their sustenance. They are, or were (Wheelwright is long dead), very dear friends of mine, but I would never claim them as America's leading poets.

The immense popularity of the Beats in Europe on both sides of the Iron Curtain is due to the fact that, although they may not reflect the eschatological emphasis of modern philosophy, they do reflect an emotional consciousness of the fact of apocalypse. What is the reason for this state of affairs? The answer is self-evident. From the death of Longfellow to the day Allen Ginsberg took off his clothes, the American poet was not an important factor in American life. He was not a factor at all. For this reason, the kind of young man who wished to participate in the decisions of his community went into business, engineering, or the professions. The boy who knew he could not or was afraid to participate wrote verse.

A generation or so ago the poet considered himself an outcast because he partook only minimally of the life of his society. Today he is very much an incast. Society has overtaken and surpassed him. Everybody gets very little out of life nowadays. The engineer who once went off in kepi, breeches, and puttees to build roads through the haunts of the headhunters now lives in a garden suburb, finds his sexual outlet in Saturday night dirty-movies parties, and for maximized living reads *On the Road* and subscribes to *The Evergreen Review*. His indistinguishable neighbor teaches creative poetry at the local college and writes slide-rule poems more indistinguishable still. What is wrong with the vast bulk of American society is that it is smug. The neurosis of the affluent society is not anxiety but *taedium vitae*—*accidie*—moral boredom.

Over the years since the First War there have been a number of poets who have given expression to certain general ideas of more or less social importance for our time. A list of them makes curious reading—Vachel Lindsay put into one-time immensely popular doggerel the mystic Midwest Populism that had come down from the communitarian experiments of the 1840's—Robert Owen and so on, and which found final expression in the sentimental manifestoes of Louis Sullivan and Frank Lloyd Wright. Eliot's *The Waste Land* is the only major work of "anxiety" in American poetry. Conrad Aiken was one of the very few writers anywhere before the surrealists to attempt to use psychoanalysis as a basic philosophy of life. The surrealists themselves were passionate evangelists of a dogmatic world view, which presumed to use art, in the words of André Breton, "to revolutionize the human sensibility as such." Eugène Jolas, the editor of *transition,* was a more learned man and a more ambitious thinker than Breton himself. Unfortunately, the whole program was fundamentally misconceived and resulted in poetry which today seems trivial and dull. The best long surrealist poem by an American was Parker Tyler's *Granite Butterfly*. Reading it over today, it simply does not seem effective enough. Hart Crane's *The Bridge* failed precisely because of its total lack of intellectual content. Hart Crane certainly led a textured enough life. But what tortured him was inability to hold a job, unhealthy relations with his parents, inability to accept his own homosexuality gracefully, and alcohol. He was not tortured by any failure of life to provide him with significance. On the contrary, he was a rather simple-minded man, gusty and lusty with a great appetite for crude experience. His most ambitious poem is an impressive attempt to write again the patriotic epic exhortations of Walt Whitman. Insofar as it fails, it does so for no profound reason, but simply because Hart Crane was not able to control his appetites. His intoxication with his own rhetoric defeats his gospel, and his poem is devoid of general ideas entirely. Other writers of long ruminative reveries (we used to call them philosophical epics) like Walter Lowenfels' *Some Deaths* or Louis Zukofsky's *A* or Charles Olson's *Maximus Poems*—in spite of all the avant-garde rhetoric—manage to say only quite conventional things. Of no one is this more true than of Gertrude Stein. A whole generation thought she must be deep because no one believed that anybody could take so much trouble to say such fatuous things as she seemed on the face of it to be saying. Late in life she suddenly started to write conventional English and revealed herself as possessed of the most extraordinarily ordinary intellectual endowment. Properly understood, she bears a strong resemblance to her contemporary, Edgar Guest. Who reflects the "age of anxiety" which is so much the concern of French intellectuals, German theologians, and American psychiatrists? W. H. Auden wrote a book called that. But W. H. Auden is English; his state of anxiety has conspicuously died down in the last few years, and he's considered very out of date. Leonard Bernstein wrote a symphony called *The Age of Anxiety* but I don't think the things that make him anxious could be classed as ontological *Angst*. It's perfectly true that George Barker, Dylan Thomas, Auden, David Gascoyne do give utterance to the kind of metaphysical terror which afflicts many people who confront the ultimate implications of the contemporary human condition. They are all British. Thomas is dead; the rest are middle-aged and not read by young English poets. "The Movement," so-called, which dominates English verse is not a movement at all. It is simply a reflection of the fact that English poets in recent years have, like their American counterparts, become well-paid professors of creative writing. Anything more flaccid and less creative it would be difficult to imagine. There are certain American poets, like Robert Lowell or Robert Creeley, whose work is haunted by anxiety, but this is, in each case, an individual psychological problem and very far from a judgment as to the meaning of life. This is the trouble with the most alienated of the Beats. Their alienation is a luxury product of the affluent society. They can afford to live in what Lawrence Lipton calls voluntary poverty (viz. no fourth TV set in the bathroom). Villon, Baudelaire, Van Gogh could not afford it and that's all the difference.

Does this mean that I think American poetry in the twentieth century is worthless? Quite the contrary. It serves society as it always has, as a symbolic criticism of value, but the values it concerns itself with are not those of philosophy or a metaphysics of the conscience. The one specifically philosophic American poet of the twentieth century has been Wallace Stevens and his work has been a kind of versification of the philosophy of George Santayana, of what Santayana called skepticism and animal faith. But Stevens' poetry is not of the great artistic merit that it is because it versifies Santayana. If that's what we want, it's better to go the original in Santayana's own prose. What is valuable about the poetry of Wallace Stevens is that it really does reorganize the human sensibility afresh in each poem in terms of quite simple elements of experience. This experience is never more profound than that accessible to the kind of man Wallace Stevens in fact was—a wealthy cultivated executive of a big insurance company.

So with William Carlos Williams, who for contemporary taste

tion of the neo and post-Beats of the unprintable school, who are incorrigibly bare-bottomed boys with cheeks of tan, the last five years of American poetry give the impression of being is the best of the generation of Classic Modernists. As a handler of general ideas, Williams is pathetic. As either esthetic or epistemology, his favorite phrase, "No ideas but in things," is infantile. He thought of his great poem *Paterson* as a philosophic epic preaching precisely that profound philosophy. What it is, of course, is a profound organization of the life experience of a small-town doctor with all of a small-town doctor's infinite roots into a community into which he was born, practiced medicine, and never left except for vacations. To products of environments as troubled as those which produced Rilke, Maiakofsky, Paul Éluard, or Dylan Thomas, even the most tormented American poet must seem singularly content, but so it is.

1965

8.

Poetry and Money

As I did to gather information about the young poets, so for this companion piece on the economics of poetry I sent out questionnaires. Some of these questions may seem a bit ingenuous—or disingenuous—but they are to reveal certain recalcitrant problems that beset poetry publishing.

Fifty per cent of the publishers say they publish one or two titles a year. Twenty-five per cent said none. Interestingly, the largest commercial publishers and the small avant-garde specialists (10 per cent of those queried) average the same number yearly—five. In addition, there are a few small publishing houses which publish only poetry. Of these the highest number of titles was 11.

In most cases this was not a set proportion, although some publishers admitted to a very definite set proportion of poetry titles as a matter of policy—that is, none. A few years ago there were several regular poetry series. None of these has survived except with the university presses and the avant-garde specialists.* Only these houses and two others have regular poetry editors. In three firms which do not publish poetry at all, fairly well-known minor poets of the Thirties are now senior editors and answered the questionnaire with sad irony. Most publishers who publish poetry use well-known poets and critics as readers. James Laughlin of New Directions and Alan Swallow of Alan Swallow pick their own poets and seldom rely on outside advice. The same is true of Lawrence Ferlinghetti's Pocket Poets. Corinth's Totem list is edited by LeRoi Jones. The Yale Series of Younger Poets is always edited by a poet. Denise Levertov was until recently editor of a similar list.

First orders for an average book of verse range from 250 to 5000. Maximum reprint orders are probably 25,000 for Ferlinghetti's *Coney Island of the Mind* with New Directions, and the same for *Howl* with the Pocket Poets. The great majority of publishers print 2000 and then simply do not reprint unless the book is a fantastic success. Given the conditions of trade publishing overhead, especially if the publisher's office is in New York, and he uses a warehouse in the vicinity, this is not a break-even point, at any possible retail price. However, this is misleading. If the general overhead is thought of as carrying the poetry on which usually little or nothing except the printer's bill is spent specifically, the book does not lose money if it sells out. Alan Swallow, one of the most dedicated of all poetry publishers, answers this question with great intelligence:

"Break-even point is an invention of commercial publishers, who assign to each book certain costs—usually those of production, a certain share of editorial costs, and a percentage of return for overhead of selling, et cetera. As a general rule, one cannot make such assignments and sell enough poetry to break even, book after book. A few will; most will not. And pay royalties, too, of course.

"Since it is true that one cannot pay commercial prices for production (let alone assign these other costs) and pay royalties —and sell enough to bring back all out-of-pocket expense, for say 80 per cent or so of the books of poetry published, my

* This is no longer true and there are now many.

answer for 25 years has been simple: I reduce the out-of-pocket expense of production by doing much-to-most of my own production; I assign to the title only those expenses, including royalties, which are encumbered thus, plus any other direct expense, such as particular advertising, promotion, etc., that can be divided from the normal, general, continuous promotion of my entire list. Under such a plan, one can bring out a book of 100 copies and break even if he has to."

The trick is to create a kind of financial enclave within the production system of a regular trade house, a kind of Alan Swallow subsidiary. This in fact is what most publishers do. Then the problem reduces itself to one of warehousing. The print order must be kept small enough so the book will sell out. New Directions solved this problem for years by refusing to remainder any poetry titles and storing them in the barn on the publisher's farm. Today even the soiled returns of first editions of those poets who sold so poorly before the war now bring collector's prices. Low overhead is the advantage enjoyed by most university presses. Besides, several of them have been recipients of foundation grants for the publishing of contemporary poetry.

Most publishers do not have any poet whom they reprint year after year, like Frost, Millay, Benton, Dylan Thomas, Alice Duer Miller, Ferlinghetti, Ginsberg. Interestingly enough, the translations of Garcia Lorca rank amongst the very highest sellers. As far as I can determine, the maximum is reached by Ferlinghetti and Ginsberg, both of whom have long since passed the quarter-million mark in America alone. Anthology permissions, foreign publication and translation, various other fees make up a small but steady income for both poet and publisher if the poet becomes well known.

If the larger trade houses do publish much poetry, they feed it in to the regular promotion and sales machinery just like other general titles. Some few advertise poetry in newspaper book-review sections, in specialized magazines like *Poetry,* and aid the poet in booking readings and lectures, if he wishes. The oral presentation of poetry has become so popular in recent years that most poets of any standing have more dates of this kind than they can handle.

A surprising number of publishers answered the question, "Does anybody in your office read poetry for pleasure?" with an unqualified, "No." Others, a minority, with an enthusiastic yes—often the general editor or publisher himself. However, appended general remarks and answers to the question, "Who are your own favorite living poets?" and to my tenth question, which I wish to discuss next, sometimes reveal an astonishing ignorance, bad taste, or active hostility; and one, but only one, questionnaire came back, anonymously, scribbled in a crabbed hand and full of personal abuse from a publishing house, whatever it was, which had not published any poetry in forty years.

The great mystery in the publishing of poetry is not the unprofitability of good poetry, once it gets published, but the difficulty it has of getting published in the first place, and the astonishing bulk of mediocre, utterly characterless verse that does get published, year after year. This is not only true in America and England, but contrary to popular belief, it is true in France and Germany as well. For this reason I asked the following question in an effort to try to uncover the source of the prevailing bad taste in choices of first volumes of verse:

Question 10: "It is an unfortunate fact that a great deal of the poetry published in America, especially by the larger publishers, is mediocre and does not sell at all, while the important poets who do sell steadily down the years are published, at least in the first instance, by non-commercial publishers, university presses, and the avant-garde specialists. This is true, though the poetry itself may be quite conventional. Do you have any theory as to why this is so?"

Most respondents simply denied the assumptions of the question, but from disparate and contradictory points of view. Others were honestly misinformed about literary history. The outstanding exceptions are cummings, first published by Boni (after *8 Harvard Poets*), Hart Crane, first published by Liveright, Wallace Stevens, first published by Knopf. Without exception these books were remaindered. I still have my copies bought at remainder prices. In fact, I bought 100 copies of Stevens's *Harmonium* at 25 cents each. Here is a representative selection of answers to Question 10:

University Presses

"We do not publish original American or English poetry, but only translations. No theory on the phenomenon mentioned, but we note that some university presses have had good advice and have published good poets, while others (whom we won't name) have a record of mediocrity. We have refrained from starting a series such as those mentioned above largely because we have not seen a clear and workable method of avoiding the mediocrity you mention. Perhaps a state university press is not the best place for the publication of original poetry. By limiting ourselves to translations, we can maintain a surer (or more nearly sure) control over quality."

"I suppose that this reflects the feeling that poetry is too marginal an economic proposition to be worth serious attention. Also, there is in contemporary poetry such a wide range of styles, such diversity of schools, that editors and publishers tend to be uncertain of their ability to choose; they either avoid doing so at all, or chose conventionally. The best poetry will continue to be introduced by the non-commercial publishers, to the extent that their owners and editors feel strongly enough about individual poets, or the obligation to give poets a chance in print, to back their own preferences and handle the economic problems as best they can."

"I have an additional impression that poetry at the present time is passing through a period of experiment, above all the experiment of trying to see how much of reality can be presented 'poetically'—that is, organized from a point of view infused with intelligent passion—while disregarding the cosmetics, hair do's, and rehearsed postures inherited from the past. This fine and necessary experiment has resulted in some losses, through discarding too much of the inherited legitimate resources of poetry in the determination to 'walk naked,' and has not yet (or so I think) produced the exceptional poets under forty who may yet appear. In this sense, the contemporary poetic scene may be described as lively and promising, but perhaps not as arresting, not as imperatively interesting in its interpretation of our lives, as we want it to be."

"The works of the poets whom you regard as important, although they may sell steadily down the years, may sell at a low rate. A university publisher is likely to think that the publication of excellent poetry is a natural part of his role, even though it means a financial loss."

"Publishers are notoriously ignorant where poetry is concerned and do not trust their judgment. Therefore they must depend on experts who are often 'big names,' established poets. This is especially unfortunate, since established poets either have pets that they push or are just humane. Many a mediocre poet comes to a publisher with lots of sweet things said about his work by name poets; commercial publishers occasionally will do one of their novelists' 'slim vols' of poetry just to keep him happy. If you are equating good poets with important poets, I don't think the evidence supports the view that non-commercial publishers have been any better than the commercial in finding talent. It's mostly an accident. Commercial boys may steer away from experimental type of stuff more."

". . . As you have pointed out yourself, a great deal of mediocre verse is being published and one of the results is that those who have the determination to seek out the best stuff have to spend all their time sorting like mail clerks. Publishers are very conscious of 'prestige.' They want a list that 'looks good' and the cheapest way to make one's list look good is to throw in a slim volume of new verse. It only costs $2000 and you don't have to take any trouble editing it. Neither do you have to spend any money promoting it since you can always fall back on the explanation that poetry never sells. But the publisher is left with a nice feeling that he has paid his dues to the Muse. . . .

"Literary reputations frequently are made or begin in academic circles. Many poets are teaching and on campuses with university presses."

"We are aware that it is difficult to build a good poetry list. Therefore we have decided not to enter into competition with other university presses which have considerable strength in this field. Rather, we have published heavily in other humanistic areas with seeming equal need for publication outlet, including books of criticism on poets such as cummings, Stevens, Eliot, and Thomas, and an anthology."

"Despite your mentioning ours as 'prestige' items (attributing this opinion to us), we are serious about publishing poetry—and do not simply publish an occasional book of verse, at a predictable loss, to balm our souls or to make a gesture to culture or to create a tax loss. Perhaps if our motives were different, we wouldn't work so hard at keeping the quality up. All this assumes that what you have said is true—which I think is open to discussion."

"Another way of saying what you've said is, I think, that many first books are published by a variety of publishers, but that the important poets ultimately are published by the larger publishers. What's wrong with that? The fact that many young poets (and novelists and artists, etc.) do not fulfill their promise is axiomatic. Those who do succeed become true literary properties; the non-commercial, university press, and avant-garde publishers cannot then compete (if they even should) with the larger publishers."

"I certainly don't object to publishing (not necessarily here, however!) mediocre poets so long as the good ones are published too. And *that* is, to my mind, the trick: cast the net wide enough to catch genius."

"Most young poets of promise teach or have some connection with a university."

Specialists

"Is this completely true? cummings, after *8 Harvard Poets,* was first published by Boni, then by Cape, then Seltzer. Wallace Stevens' first book was published by Knopf; there are exceptions. I would suggest that, especially since Wall Street has invaded publishing, poetry has been ignored as non-commercial—not good business. First books of poetry are traditionally slight and their possible sales would not warrant investment in publicity. When prestige or corporate image requires the publication of a certain proportion of poetry titles, I believe that editors who are non-discriminating and who have no serious interest in poetry will choose only traditional, conventional, obvious, non-controversial material. The choice of a specific poet or book of poetry by a major publisher is undoubtedly an accidental, chancy thing."

"There is only one reason to publish poetry, and that is a conviction of taste."

Trade

". . . In the Great Society in which we are all caught today, it would have to warrant a printing of 5000 copies to begin with and that, I fear, would not be possible with most of the poetry I see today. But I shall continue to read and hope . . ."

"Many trade publishers, I'd guess, publish poetry only as an adjunct—if a novelist or a writer of non-fiction they repeatedly publish, wants a volume of verse brought out, they'll do it. But being neither attuned to poetry nor convinced they can distribute it except at a loss, they do not seek it out."

"Trade presses don't want to bother with short-run books . . . From the editorial point of view some poets—the ones who have not previously had a collection published—are a real headache to work with: letters or phone calls practically daily for months. And time is money, even though we can't figure into the cost of a book all the time that is wasted dislodging the poet from our hair.

"I hope your article will clarify just what you mean by these generalizations, which seem to me to be, at best, half truths."

"No."

"Important poets start as unimportant, hence ones generally ignored by larger houses—hence find first publication with small presses."

"My theory is that poets, like painters, musicians, sculptors, dancers, etc., have gone so private that the public puts up a defense and rejects them completely even when potentially they might well enjoy them or some of them, or aspects of some of them. Maybe the poetry readings will re-establish contact."

"I just don't agree that this is so. I think that first books of poetry usually don't have enormous sales quite certainly, but I don't think that necessarily means they are mediocre and I would have thought that the important poets were published by larger publishers from the beginning. It's possible that I'm wrong about this; the people I've followed from the very beginning have been the agent Curtis Brown's authors, such as Auden and Spender, who certainly were published by larger publishers from the beginning [Note by K. R.: They weren't in England.], the people I've worked with. We published A——— first and B———, and we think they're good no matter what other people might think. Both these people would seem to me to be serious poets who are going to sell in the future. Were we not the first publishers of R———? It's true that C———, whose second book we are doing, was published first by ——— State and D——— by University of ——— [Note by K. R.: This man in fact was first published by himself, then by small California presses, then by a cooperative in a conscientious objectors' camp. Finally his eighth but first hardcover book was published by the oldest avant-garde specialist—on my persistent recommendation. It took ten years of steady nagging to get the woman who is now universally recognized as America's leading post-war poet accepted by even an avant-garde house.], but in neither case were we offered the work of these poets until their first book had been taken. I don't know what the story is on C——— but D——— knew the University of ——— people and did not try to get his book published elsewhere except possibly by the large avant-garde houses, which would be in the same category in any case. I think if there is any theory that I hold it is that frequently young poets don't realize that they have as good a chance to be published by a large house that does go in for poetry as by anybody else.

"Far too many theories, but suspect you've thought of them all."

"We question the premise of this inquiry. There is nothing non-commercial about university presses in today's publishing—at least among the better ones."

"The publication of poetry—that is, good poetry of quality, no matter the trend—requires a dedicated publisher—and these don't come in the commercial field as a rule. Poetry does not show on the stock exchange, nor in dividends, nor in profits. Lucky if cost of production is retrieved in the course of a few years. We were surprised to sell out half an edition of our anthology of new poetry within the first five months of publication. But we took the precaution of putting it into cheaper paperback edition at the same time as the cloth. Nevertheless, we intend to publish more poetry."

"The economics of poetry publishing is that a book by an American poet, except the half-dozen famous ones, will sell 600–1000 copies in the trade edition and incur a certain loss of $3–4000 for the publisher. Publishers expect poetry to lose money. If they publish poetry (except for the few widely accepted poets) they regard the money lost as contributions to a conscience fund."

"Difficulty of judging marketability of poetry. Commercial publishers cannot afford to gamble frequently."

So much for the publishers, now for the poets. How do poets live? Do any of them live exclusively off their poetry? Do many live by writing at all? If not, what do they do? The answers are simple. Only Allen Ginsberg lives exclusively on his poetry, from royalties and readings. Most of Ogden Nash's income comes from his poetry. Langston Hughes lives by writing, but he makes more money from the theater than from poetry. I live by writing but most of this income is from highbrow journalism. We are the only ones I've been able to find.

I doubt if Ginsberg's income exceeds the first rung of the income tax ladder. I have excluded persons dependent on their spouses. There are a couple of housewives who could probably support themselves from their poetry, notably Phyllis McGinley, and there are a number of young bohemians who live on their wives or mistresses—male or female—but this is a region where sociological inquiry would constitute an invasion of privacy and lead to meager and misleading results.

Most American poets, including the avant-garde and those under thirty-five, are academicians. Robert Creeley, Denise Levertov, and LeRoi Jones are just as much part of the establishment as Archibald MacLeish or Robert Lowell. Salaries for poets teaching routine English courses or creative writing, or occupying Chairs of Poetry, range from $4000 a year to over $20,000. These salaries, except at the very top, are often for a full load of teaching. Some poets teach only just enough to get by. Others are teaching assistants and in some schools are paid very little, and in a few paid nothing. For holders of fellowships the minimum is about $600. This minimum may seem astonishingly low but we forget about the small colleges in the American Balkans.

A few poets—John Ciardi, Robert Lowell, Lawrence Ferlinghetti are examples—could live modestly on their income from poetry alone if they so chose. My own royalties from poetry alone average $200 a month, year in, year out, and I suppose I could live on it if I didn't have a family. All sorts of people do. This is about a median income from royalties for a successful poet—a little more than most of the older establishment whose books in fact do not sell very well, and a little less than the new establishment, some of whom sell very well indeed.

A few poets live by work in no way related to literature. The outstanding examples a generation ago were William Carlos Williams, a successful small city doctor, and Wallace Stevens, a wealthy insurance executive. There are fewer and fewer people of this kind. The population explosion, the culture explosion, and the education explosion have overwhelmed the seceders from society at the bottom and the gentlemen of letters at the top. The demand for the services which the poet can provide society is simply too great to permit withdrawal.

Archibald MacLeish, if he chose, could certainly be a very successful lawyer and "write on the side" as he did in his youth. For years he held the most prestigious literary-academic job in the country. Before that he was Librarian of Congress. Richard Eberhart resigned from an executive position in business to take a poetry chair at Dartmouth. At the other end of the economic scale, Gary Snyder, who is a Zen monk, has taught at the University of California. Philip Whalen, who has always lived on minimum part-time jobs, is now teaching English in Japan. The largest percentage of people living by ordinary jobs and writing poetry is probably to be found amongst young Negro poets, but here academic demand far exceeds supply.

There is no reason why poets should not work as columnists, critics, and highbrow journalists generally, as they do in France. The newspapers and magazines would be glad to get them, but the social alienation which goes with the practice of poetry in America has prevented the poet from developing skills of this kind. To the best of my knowledge I am the only person in the United States who writes anything like "Les Bloc-Notes" of François Mauriac except Norman Mailer's column in *The Village Voice*. I guess it's a long time since Norman wrote much poetry.

No important American poet at the present time makes a living writing fiction. The last person to do this successfully was the English poet, C. Day Lewis, who wrote detective stories under another name, and Henry Treece, who wrote historical novels. The fact that these people are English points to the reason it is not done in America. American publishing of fiction is so obnoxiously commercialized that it is repugnant to the type of sensibility that turns to poetry. Then, too, there is another objection the poet has to living by writing of any kind. As Moses said to the lady who asked how he grew such a beautiful beard, "I don't shave every day."

Whether the cause is the American tax structure, guilty conscience, or genuine benevolence, we now live in a time of foundation explosion, too. There are more foundations today in America giving away money than there are worthy recipients and the givers miss most of the latter. The commonest American abroad is *le foundation bum,* nasalized and pronounced as in French. There are quite a few people who write verse who manage to go from foundation grant to foundation grant never touching ground, and unlike Antaeus, ever gathering strength. Although it's possible to retire for life to the Greek isles on the savings from a series of cleverly managed grants, the verse produced by these people never seems to be much good, except for one woman who is one of America's better poets and who to the best of my knowledge has not been un-granted since 1945.

So much for the economics of the practice of poetry as we have always known it. Outside this world altogether a new kind of poetry is growing up in a new kind of society. Poetry plays as important a role as music in the ever-proliferating subculture which challenges The American Way of Life at every point—the New Youth, the New Left—the mass disaffiliation which so frightens the writers of sociological editorials.

Political organizations that represent one pole or the other of the vast evil try to use this subculture without success. Turnouts like the great Vietnam protests are not led by Trotskyites-Maoists on the Vietnam Day Committee, but tailed by them, and it is significant that the apparatchiki cannot get along with the poets of protest and much prefer the mediocre academicians who satisfy tastes shared by Mao, Khrushchev, and Trotsky.

It is the essence of the culture of the disestablishment that it is self-supporting. It publishes—or utters—itself. Its producers are its consumers and vice versa. It has no market problems.

The myth is: The publishing of poetry in America has always been governed by rigid preconceptions: (1) It does not pay. (2) It confers prestige on a publisher's list. (3) The kind of people who get jobs as publisher's readers are capable of selecting it. (4) Nobody reads that avant-garde poetry which doesn't make any sense like Gertrude Stein and Maxwell Bodenheim. (5) What the public wants and would buy in large quantities if it were offered them is that nice, old-timey poetry which rhymes and which is so easy to understand, like Keats's Odes and Shakespeare's Sonnets.

The facts are: (1) Poetry does sell. (2) Since its production costs are cheaper than prose, if it sells at all it's very profitable.

(3) Much of the poetry published by the large publishing houses is written by married and unmarried maiden ladies of both sexes and only makes for a moment of levity in publishers' catalogues. (4) This must be due to the fact that few people connected with publishing read poetry, or read at all, for pleasure. Good poets appear in the lists of most big publishers by accident, and are usually dropped after one book. Most of them are published because the publisher hopes to persuade the poet to write a novel, even though anthropology or archeology are today safer bets than fiction, and good poetry that any cultivated person could pick is safer than either of them. (5) Only avant-garde poetry sells or ever has—except Robert Frost, Edna St. Vincent Millay, Alice Duer Miller. Only Frost of these three sold steadily till the end of his life, while *Leaves of Grass* has sold out edition after edition year after year from the day of its publication to the present. Ogden Nash could hardly be called a conventional poet. True, he rhymes. But when? But how?

1965

9.
The Heat

Recently police activity began to impinge upon my own life. I live in a San Francisco Negro district and I could see about me a noticeable increase—prowl cars were more evident at all times. On weekend nights they seemed to be everywhere, stopping and questioning many more people than formerly.

An art gallery was raided and welded sculpture illustrating the *Kama Sutra* was confiscated by the police. This was entirely a police action without civilian complaint. The police lost the case. Student parties in San Francisco's Haight-Ashbury district were raided again and again and everybody hauled off to jail. Even where the police claim to have found marihuana butts on the floor, the cases were usually dismissed. In New York two parties of the Artists' and Writers' Committee Against Vietnam, a group with no political affiliations, were raided without a warrant or complaint and several arrests made.

Friends of mine married to members of another race began to complain that they were frequently stopped by prowl cars and questioned when walking along the street with their spouses in broad daylight. After the Ginzburg decision there was a noticeable increase throughout the country in police censorship; in San Francisco bookshops were visited by police officers who told the proprietors, "Clean this place up or we'll take you in," but vouchsafed no information as to what books were in fact objectionable.

Certain costumes seem to be an open invitation to police questioning—beards, dirty jeans, bare feet, especially on juveniles, but more commonly still the uniform of the homosexual prostitute, the studbuster—T-shirt, leather jacket, tight jeans, heavy belt, boots. I began to get all sorts of complaints: a well-known jazz musician taking a breather in front of a perfectly respectable jazz room between sets and talking to his white wife was arrested, taken to the local station, held for two hours, insulted, and then let go. Another driving with his wife was arrested for a minor traffic violation, failure to signal a right-hand turn, and taken to the station.

No policemen had molested me in over forty years. I drink only wine at dinner. Marihuana has no effect on me. I haven't smoked it since adolescence. I am a very safe driver. However subversive my opinions, I am an exemplary law-abiding citizen. However, one night I parked my car in front of my own home, took my two daughters to the door, left my secretary in the car. When I returned the police, who obviously thought they were dealing with a racially mixed couple, had been questioning my secretary and because they hadn't liked the tone of her voice were writing a traffic ticket.

In the next block the same patrol had threatened a neighbor with arrest in a similar situation. A few blocks away a Negro youth leader had an appointment for lunch with a police officer. On the way to the lunch he was rousted by that very officer. A Negro high-school boy acting in a school play with my daughter was stopped as he was walking home from rehearsal along a well-lighted business street, rousted, and eventually forced to lie down on the sidewalk, but finally let go.

All of this happened in my immediate neighborhood, to people known to me, in one month. Yet San Francisco's police force is unquestionably one of the most professional in the country, with the extremely active community-relations detail led by a dedicated officer, an enlightened chief, lectures and classes on civil liberties, race relations, youth problems, and like matters. Reports in the press and from friends in other cities of increasing petty police harassment were far more shocking. It was apparent that The Heat was on—nationally. Why?

What exactly is The Heat and what turns it on? And why should it suddenly go on all over the country? The documentation of police brutality and violation of civil liberties in various cities about the country is staggering. But this is not what I want to write about.

In recent months there have been a number of magazine articles and serial newspaper features on "What's Wrong With the Police," and these have been answered in most cases by literate spokesmen for the police, not PR men, but working officers themselves. There's very little dialogue. One side makes flat accusations, usually well-documented, of police brutality, illegal entry or search, harassment, prejudice against the poor, racism, political reaction, third-degree, and other violations of the rights of those arrested. The other side simply denies that most of these things exist, and counters with the statement, "Police work is a profession with very special problems which the layman cannot understand any more than he can understand the special problems of medicine or law."

Both sides isolate the problem and treat the police as though they were members of a self-contained society—separate from the rest of us, like monks, professional soldiers, or the inmates of prisons and state hospitals. The problem is the functioning of the police as part of society, not as apart from it. Essential to any understanding is the definition of the roles that the police perform in the society in fact and the different roles which they are supposed to perform in theory, their own theories and those of their critics.

The following article recently appeared in *The Berkeley Barb*:

POLICE RAID NUDE FEST . . . LIKE "GANGBUSTERS"

Berkeley police with flashbulbs blazing ran swiftly through a gathering of about 40 nude men and women last Saturday. They were "investigating" possible lawbreaking at an East Bay Sexual Freedom League party. "It was like "Gangbusters'," EBSFL President Richard Thorne told BARB.

"They came in very quickly and told us to hold it, stay where we were, and flashed cameras." The police searched the house and checked the I.D. of each guest. They stayed for about an hour, around midnight. "After I got dressed, I went to the lieutenant in charge and inquired on what grounds the police were present," Thorne said. "The lieutenant said that someone had issued a complaint which led them to suspect that there was the possibility of contributing to the delinquency of minors. " 'Of what sort?' I asked him. "He said, "Alcohol'." Thorne and several other witnesses described the police investigation. Desks, chairs, bureaus, and clothes in closets were searched. Ashtrays were examined. Medicines were confiscated. Brown filipino cigarettes were peeled open. Guests who objected to showing their I.D.'s were given the choice of cooperating or being identified "at the station." At BARB presstime, no arrests had resulted from the investigation. One guest, who met a flashbulb as he emerged from the bathroom, described his conversation with the plainclothesman who apparently admitted the other police:

"I asked him what had happened to give them the right to enter and search without a warrant.

"He said, 'Are you a lawyer?'

"I said, 'No.'

" 'In that case, it's none of your business,' he said." Witnesses described the police demeanor as initially "rude," "sarcastic," "snide," and "up tight." As the hour passed, they "settled down" and became "mannerly" and "courteous," guests said. About 20 partygoers remained after the police departed. "Clothes came off again at a rapid rate after they left," one participant told BARB. "It was as if they wouldn't let the police intimidate them, and they wanted to release a pent-up rage. It became quite a party. A very fine, successful party."

Following the publication of this article I took it upon myself to question one of the members of the Berkeley Police Force regarding the matter. Our conversation was friendly and was not confined to the police raid although it covered the pertinent aspects. Pertinent portions of the interview were in sum and substance to this effect:

INTERVIEWER: What happened at the nude party?
POLICE OFFICER: Oh, we alleged that there were people below the age of 18 there but there weren't.
I: Did you really believe that there was someone below the age of 18?
P: No, we just used that as an excuse.
I: Well, what happened?
P: We busted into the place and there were several couples actually fornicating. So, we took some pictures and left.
I: What did you do with the pictures?

P: Oh, they're fun to pass around for all the boys to look at down at the station.
I: Isn't that illegal?
P: Well, I suppose so but they were having a nude party.
I: Didn't the attorney general of the state of California specifically say that nude parties were legal?
P: Oh, we know that there isn't anything illegal going on, but we feel that if you let this kind of thing happen it's like opening Pandora's Box.
I: Is the police department supposed to prescribe morals?
P: Somebody's got to.
I: Doesn't the Constitution of the United States specifically allow the citizenry to determine its own morals?
P: Well, you know how these things are.
I: Would you want the police busting into your home under these circumstances?
P: Well, I wouldn't be doing anything illegal.
I: Neither were they.

This example, however comic, poses the dilemma: the contradiction between the police as officers of order and officers of law. In the early days of the development of modern police forces perhaps their primary function was the preservation of social order and the enforcement of public morality. They dealt mostly with the poor, who, however unruly, accepted the same values. In a heterogeneous society such as America was in the days of massive immigration, most of the work of a patrolman on the beat in Hell's Kitchen, the lower East Side, Five Points, Back of the Yards, was extra-legal. He was not a law officer but a peace officer and if he invoked the law to handle all violations of public order he would have found himself hopelessly overwhelmed. Until recent years the Paris police force still operated this way in almost all their day-to-day work. The vicious, disorderly, the conspicuous violaters of common morals, were simply taken up an alley and "coated" with a weighted cape or worked over with a truncheon and kicked out on the street with a warning that if they were caught doing it again they'd get worse in the station house.

Vice (prostitution, gambling, narcotics) as distinguished from crime was "policed." Streetwalkers were protected on their stations from invasion by other whores or pimps, and guarded against robbery or attack by their customers. This type of relationship—which was usually effective—was always advanced in private conversation by American policemen as an excuse for payoff: "If you clout them, you control them." It still prevails in the Tenderloin districts of many American cities.

America has changed. It is becoming a homogeneous society and the divisions that do exist are of a new kind. First, of course, is the conflict over homogeneity itself to which the Negroes demand they be admitted. The second most important division, from the police point of view, is a change of values, the democratization of what was once the privilege of an élite of radical intellectuals—an entirely new moral code. Emma Goldman, free-lover and anarchist, was quite a sufficient bother to the police of her day. Today there are millions of Emma Goldmans, members of a new kind of middle class. This public resents the police as guardians of public morals. Younger people who live by moral codes which bear little resemblance to the lower-middle-class Irish Catholic morality of most of the police force look upon the policeman as a dangerous and ignorant disrupter of their own peaceful lives.

The police on the other hand believe that they have the right to control the lives of others for their own benefit, that they know better what others should do than they do themselves. They adjust the behavior of those who live by a different moral code to the stereotypes which they have inherited from the past. In its most extreme form: "If you see a nigger and a white woman together, chances are it's a pimp and a whore." "All those beatniks," referring to a bearded student of nuclear physics, "take dope." "If you watch you can catch one of them making a pass and you're sure to find marihuana or pills."

Both press and police commonly refer to marihuana, an intoxicant far less harmful than alcohol, and to LSD and the various barbiturates, tranquilizers, and stimulants as "dope" and "narcotics," and attempt to deal with the problem exactly the same way that they dealt with the morphine traffic and addiction of fifty years ago. It is significant that the use of most of these drugs results in relaxation and non-invasive behavior while alcohol stimulates aggressions. The police as the Arm of the Squares represent an aggressive lower-middle-class morality in conflict with life patterns of non-aggression which they find incomprehensible and interpret in terms of crime and vice—aggression—which they *can* understand.

What is it the spokesmen for the police are talking about when they say the public doesn't understand the nature of police work? Why don't they explain? The reason is that the contradiction, the dilemma of police work, is something they do not wish publicized. They wish to present to a society concerned about civil liberties the policeman as a functionary of the legal process. They are not prepared to face the fact that he is involved in a symbiotic relationship within the illegal communities that function as subcultures in the society.

It is a common charge of those interested in a reform of the methods of handling the narcotic problem that the federal, state, and, to a lesser degree, city police have a "vested interest," along with the Mafia, in preserving the status quo. This is an oversimplification. What has actually developed is a great web of petty crime, addiction, peddling which the narcotics officer hopes he can control and which is sensitive to his manipulation.

For instance, to begin at the beginning of the process: A narcotics addict arrested on a petty larceny charge can cooperate with the police in several ways. He can help clear the record by admitting to a number of unsolved petty thefts and he can give information which will lead to the arrest of his retail dealer, and his anonymity will be protected by the police and the charges against him will be reduced to a minimum. In the somewhat bigger time a felony charge can be reduced if the prisoner is willing to cooperate in the arrest of a narcotics wholesaler.

At the bottom of the ladder a prostitute known to have associates who are either thieves or narcotics pushers or both can cooperate simply by giving general information, or in cases where the police know that the girl has information they want, she is often given the choice between cooperation, being admitted to bail, and receiving only a fine at her trial, or refusing to cooperate, being held without bail for a medical examination, and then given a jail sentence.

All this is done with a great deal of indirection and evasive language but since narcotics control is something which the police must originate themselves—it is one of several "crimes without plaintiff" which is another definition of "vice"—gambling, prostitution and narcotics—the police can function only if they can keep a complicated machinery of information and actual social contact operating. And the fuel which keeps this machine going is bargaining power: each side has a commodity to exchange of value to the other. Each party to the transaction must make a profit. In this sense the police have a vested interest in the subculture of the underworld.

The remarkable thing about this subculture is that, although it may use the term "square," both police and criminals share the same system of value. The narcotics peddler, the gambler, or the prostitute may point out that their activities are civil-service occupations in some countries and if the public didn't want what they had to offer, they would go out of business. To some extent most policemen share this point of view, but both sides in private conversation usually will be found to be convinced that vice is morally wrong.

The underworld subculture does not have the self-confidence attributed to it in fiction. Again, this lack is a powerful psychological tool in the hands of the police. A prostitute who is treated by the arresting officer as "just a hard-working girl," the victim of hypocritical bluenosed laws which it is the officer's job to enforce, will be far more cooperative than a girl who feels she is being treated with contempt, most especially so because she herself has that contempt. Organizations like Synanon have made a therapeutic method out of the self-hate of the narcotics addict, but a policeman who used the language of a Synanon session would find himself with a very hostile prisoner indeed on his hands.

What the policeman does as a custodial officer within the underworld subculture is keep it abated and he applies these methods to other problems of social order.

For instance, for several years I knew a handsome young Negro intellectual who was a professional blackmailer. He would spot a wealthy young married woman slumming in bohemia, strike up an acquaintance, carry on an intellectual conversation, arouse her sympathy. After reciting T. S. Eliot at length he would divulge the information that he cried himself to sleep night after night because his skin was black and his hair was crinkly. As they parted he would thank her profusely, say that he never hoped to see her again but could he write her sometimes when the pain was more than he could bear. The exchange of letters led to an exchange of pictures and possibly even to an affair, and then one day the socialite housewife would get a telephone call that he was in a terrible jam and needed a thousand dollars that he had been offered by a newspaperman for the letters and pictures. Needless to say, journalism is no longer conducted this way but the girls usually paid up and those who were sleeping with him usually went right on doing so.

One night I was in a club in San Francisco's North Beach and watched the regular cop on the beat question only the mixed couples in the place and concentrate his hostility on this man and his new girl. As he went out the door he said to me, "O.K., Rexroth, say I'm prejudiced but what do you want me to do with that motherfucker? Go up to him and say, 'You're under arrest for blackmail'?"

Eventually this harassment may have paid off because the fellow left town for good. This instance explains a good many things. The police still believe that there are enough relationships of this kind, or worse, amongst mixed couples to justify a policy of general interrogation and of making those people who do not respond as the police think they should as uncomfortable as possible. Harassment is a method of abatement and the police consider it one which may work when there is no plaintiff or no visible commission of crime.

Take the case of homosexuality. Homosexual acts between consenting adults are no longer policed as such. The laws which the police attempt to enforce are essentially the same as those applied to heterosexuals. The bushes in parks and public toilets are not chosen by heterosexuals for sexual intercourse, and although assignations are made between men and women in bars, this has become socially acceptable in most cities, and it is usually not so obvious as the activities in a gay bar.

With the growing tolerance of homosexuality and the enormous increase in gay bars and other open manifestations of homosexuality socially, there has not only been a great increase in homosexual prostitution, especially amongst floating adolescents, but a tremendous increase in robbery and murder. Not only have a number of well-known personalities in recent years been found robbed and beaten to death in cities with a large homosexual population, but studbusting has become one of the commonest forms of "unexplained" homicide. Middle-aged men, many of them married and with children, are pulled out of the bushes dead, with a frequency the police prefer to say nothing about.

Here is the police problem. No one is going to complain. The partners in a homosexual relationship participate voluntarily. If one is robbed, he will not risk disgrace by going to the police. If he's dead, he's dead, and the circumstances of his murder provide no clue. The act itself takes only a brief time and is almost impossible to catch. So the police harass and embarrass the gay bar or the respectable-looking homosexuals frequenting parks or cruising certain well-known streets looking for "trade." The "trade," the homosexual prostitute, they make as uncomfortable as possible.

At one time entrapment was a common form of arrest, but the prejudice of the court and the public is so great that it is being abandoned. A judge is very likely to say, "What were you doing when the defendant was fondling your penis?" Besides entrapment does not catch the principal offender, the studbuster, who if he is experienced can recognize a plainclothesman no matter how plausibly disguised.

This leaves the police with degrading methods, peepholes in public toilets and such like which most officers rebel against using. Of course, in all these cases some policemen simply love this kind of work. The favorite term of contempt amongst police as in the underworld is "copperhearted." Fairy-killers and whore-hunters are not liked by their colleagues on the force, and although police will give all their skill and devotion to cracking a big case of narcotics wholesaling, most men on the narcotics detail sicken of the work with the petty addict and the round of desperation, pilfering, prostitution, squalor, and the hopelessness of changing it.

There is one outstanding factor in common in almost all

arrests for "vice." The cop must *judge* to arrest, and in court in a legal process based on contest he must stick to his guns and the *esprit de corps* of the force must back him up all the way up the chain of command. A general cannot deny his troops. This is the reason that the chain of command almost invariably seems to the public to do nothing but whitewash whenever there is a complaint no matter how grievous. It is this paramilitary ethic, not corruption, which accounts for the runaround. Except for a few cities in the East, corruption from outside is dying out. If it exists today it comes from within the force. Outside the cities that are still controlled by the Organization, policemen, let alone high-ranking officers, are no longer directly controlled by corrupt political machines or by the "Mafia."

Modern police corruption is a more subtle thing. Many police departments are controlled by intra-departmental political structures, power *apparats*. Others are the battleground of conflicting groups of this sort, but they are more likely to be generated within the department and concerned exclusively with police rank and privilege than to come from outside. In fact the tendency is to keep such things from the attention of the public, even of the apparatus of the political parties.

In the case of a liberal and enlightened police chief the increasing polarization of American society is certain to be reflected in an opposition, usually clandestine but often organized, which considers him a nigger-lover and a red and whose members do everything they can to sabotage his efforts and to back each other up all along the chain of command as high as they can go. It is this type of reactionary opposition that accounts for the apparently successful John Birch Society recruitment campaign in the police forces of America, and it is here that you can find charges of whitewash and runaround in cases of police brutality, and especially of racism.

Payoff is, as I said, part of a system for control for which many otherwise honest, old-fashioned policemen will present strong if not convincing arguments. Big-time payoff is another thing and occurs only sporadically in a few Eastern cities. Criminal corruption again arises within a police force prompted only by the generally criminal character of American society.

Rings of thieves like those uncovered a couple of years ago in two police forces usually grow out of the general "knock-down" philosophy of American enterprise, particularly in relation to insurance claims. To quote Chief Stanley R. Schrotel:

> Most policemen recognize no wrong in accepting free admissions to public entertainment, discounts on their purchases, special favors and considerations from persons of influence, or tips and gratuities for services performed in the line of their regular duty. They choose to look upon these incidents as being strictly personal matters between themselves and the donors and are unwilling to recognize that moral obligations are involved. . . . No matter how much effort is expended in minimizing the derogatory effect of the acceptance of gratuities and favors by law-enforcement officers, the practice has become so prevalent that the public generally concedes that policemen are the world's greatest "moochers." Aside from the question of the effect of the practice upon the officers' effectiveness in enforcing the law, it is a certainty that a reputation for "mooching" does not elevate the standards of the profession in the public's mind.

This picture has a certain old-time charm: the copper in pith helmet and blue Prince Albert copping an apple off the push-cart. To quote again Banton's *The Policeman in the Community,* paraphrasing Morton Stern's article, "What Makes a Policeman Go Wrong": "A former member of the Denver police department, in discussing what went wrong there, stressed that a new recruit was not accepted by his colleagues unless he conformed to their norms. When investigating a burglary in a store, police officers might put some additional articles into their pockets. Indeed, they were sometimes encouraged to do so by the owners who pointed out they would recover from the insurance company anyway." In the Cops-as-Robbers scandals of a few years back, investigation soon revealed the step-by-step process of corruption. The robbery victim, owner of a shop or warehouse, expected and encouraged the investigating officers to help themselves to a couple of mink coats or television sets to run up the insurance claim. From there it was a short step to collusion between police, burglary gang, and would-be "victim," and from there a still shorter step, the elimination of the middleman, until the police planned and carried out the robberies themselves and moved on to plain, old-fashioned robbery, without the connivance of the robbed.

The corruption that stems from gambling is a special case, although its effects are probably the most far-reaching. Few police anywhere are directly part of the organized narcotics business, and their involvement in prostitution is really trivial, however common, and mostly part of what they consider the necessary web of information. Gambling is different. Today when churches and supermarkets are gambling institutions, it is hard for the average policeman, who is likely to be an Irish Catholic whose church stages weekly bingo games, to take gambling seriously.

Payoff may start as part of the system of control, but since gambling is the major business of organized crime in America, it soon penetrates to the vitals of the police system. Since gambling is also the major bridge between politics and organized crime, it carries with it not only the corruption of vice but the additional corruption of vice-controlled politics.

Collusion with bookmakers and the proprietors of gambling rooms is turned up fairly frequently on the West Coast. Massive infection of the police department and the penetration of high-level, outside, political corruption seems to be far more common east of the Rockies. There is a psychological factor here which must be taken into account. A corrupt police force is a guilt-ridden police force, because with few exceptions policemen do believe in the lower-middle-class values even when they flout them. A guilty police force is likely to be both belligerently puritanical in its attempts to control unconventional behavior, and hostile, quick to react aggressively to any fancied assault on its own authority. Obviously, this sets up a vicious circle which goes round and round in an ever-accelerating separation of the police from the general population.

At the very best, as any honest policeman will tell you, the police live in a ghetto of their own and a great deal of the effort of the human-relations bureaus and details of the better police departments is devoted simply to getting through to the public, to breaking down the ghetto wall. But even with the best public relations the police as a subculture of their own are a garrison society. Policemen associate mostly with one another and have few civilian friends. Policemen's balls and picnics are characterized by a noisy but impoverished conviviality.

In the case of Negroes, the young man who joins the force is likely to meet with a total cutoff in his community and at the best find himself uncomfortable in his new one, the police society. A neighbor who was a graduate in law in a Southern Jim Crow university joined the force and discovered that he had even lost the friendship of his minister. After a couple of years of isolation, he quit. As a custodial officer in a Negro ghetto the policeman confronts a population in revolt to whom he is a soldier of an occupying army, as both James Baldwin and Bayard Rustin have said.

I have neglected to mention the only way in which the average citizen comes in frequent contact with the police—traffic violation. This is, as we all know, an area of continual exasperation on both sides, and one of the best things a city can do is to create a department of traffic-control officers for all violations short of crime completely divorced from the police department.

To sum up, these are the basic factors in the problem: The police are a closed community, socially isolated from the general population with a high level of irritability along the edges of contact. Police methods have developed in the day-by-day work of control of an underworld of petty crime and vice, in a period when most police work was with the poor, or at least the dwellers in slums and Tenderloin. As a control or custodial officer the typical policeman, in the words of Jerome H. Skolnick, "is inherently a suspicious person, fond of order and predictability. He reacts to stereotyped symbols of potential trouble—even oddities of dress or speech, and proceeds on the presumption of guilty, often while winking at the legal niceties of restraint in searches and arrests. Intent upon 'controlling crime,' the officer keenly resents having his results upset on the appellate level."

Skolnick found that the police feel frustrated by the court's affirmation of principles of due process, and generally consider the appellate judiciary as "traitor" to its responsibility to keep the community free from criminality.

We hear a great deal about the professionalization of the policeman from theorists and lecturers in police academies but on the part of the older or more conventional of these people, professionalism really means the development of a high degree of craft skill in playing the role described by Skolnick, a social custodial officer, with maximum efficiency and minimum social friction. This body of social servants with its own ideology and ethic is set over against a society which bears little resemblance to the one which produced it in the first place. To quote Thomas F. Adams, "Field Interrogation," *Police,* March-April, 1963:

A. Be suspicious. This is a healthy police attitude, but it should be controlled and not too obvious.
B. Look for the unusual.
    1. Persons who do not "belong" where they are observed.
    2. Automobiles which do not "look right."
    3. Businesses opened at odd hours, or not according to routine or custom.
C. Subjects who should be subjected to field interrogations.
    1. Suspicious persons known to the officers from previous arrests, field interrogations, and observations.
    2. Emaciated-appearing alcoholics and narcotics users who invariably turn to crime to pay for cost of habit.
    3. Person who fits description of wanted suspect as described by radio, teletype, daily bulletins.
    4. Any person observed in the immediate vicinity of a crime very recently committed or reported as "in progress."
    5. Known trouble-makers near large gatherings.
    6. Persons who attempt to avoid or evade the officer.
    7. Exaggerated unconcern over contact with the officer.
    8. Visibly "rattled" when near the policeman.
    9. Unescorted women or young girls in public places, particularly at night in such places as cafés, bars, bus and train depots, or street corners.
    10. "Lovers" in an industrial area (make good lookouts).
    11. Persons who loiter about places where children play.
    12. Solicitors or peddlers in a residential neighborhood.
    13. Loiterers around public rest rooms.
    14. Lone male sitting in car adjacent to schoolground with newspaper or book in his lap.
    15. Lone male sitting in car near shopping center who pays unusual amount of attention to women, sometimes continuously manipulating rearview mirror to avoid direct eye contact.
    16. Hitchhikers.
    17. Person wearing coat on hot days.
    18. Car with mismatched hub caps, or dirty car with clean license plate (or vice versa).

19. Uniformed "deliverymen" with no merchandise or truck.
20. Many others. How about your own personal experiences?

And Colin McInnes, *Mr. Love and Justice*:

The true copper's dominant characteristic, if the truth be known, is neither those daring nor vicious qualities that are sometimes attributed to him by friend or enemy, but an ingrained conservatism, and almost desperate love of the conventional. It is untidiness, disorder, the unusual, that a copper disapproves of most of all: far more even than of crime which is merely a professional matter. Hence his profound dislike of people loitering in streets, dressing extravagantly, speaking with exotic accents, being strange, weak, eccentric, or simply any rare minority—of their doing, in fact, anything that cannot be safely predicted.

Then Peter J. Connell, "Handling of Complaints by Police":

The time spent cruising one's sector or walking one's beat is not wasted time, though it can become quite routine. During this time, the most important thing for the officer to do is notice the *normal*. He must come to know the people in his area, their habits, their automobiles, and their friends. He must learn what time the various shops close, how much money is kept on hand on different nights, what lights are usually left on, which houses are vacant . . . only then can he decide what persons or cars under what circumstances warrant the appellation 'suspicious.'

All this was all right in a different world. At least the society didn't fall apart. Today what was once a mob is now a civil-rights demonstration, oddly dressed people are musicians, students, professors, members of the new professions generally (half of Madison Avenue seems to take the subway home to Greenwich Village at 5:00 P.M., shed the gray flannel suits and basic blacks, and get into costumes which the police believe are worn only by "dope fiends").

Why is the heat on all over America? For exactly the same reason it has always gone on in an American city after an outbreak of social disorder, a shocking crime, or a sudden rise in the crime rate. The police feel that they are dealing with a situation that is slipping away from their control and they are using the methods, most of them extra-legal, by which they have traditionally regained control—"discourage them and they'll go away."

Where the police once confronted unassimilated groups of

the illiterate poor, they now face an unassimilable subculture of the college educated, unassimilable certainly to their own standards. Homosexuality, once a profitable source of shakedown, and a chance to release a few sadistic repressions, is now open and in fact tolerated. There are articles in theological magazines about the church's responsibility to the homosexual and an interfaith organization to implement such responsibility—"homophile" organizations of both men and women stage national conventions addressed by notabilities in law, psychiatry, and sociology, and even by a few enlightened police officers. Such organizations recently sued the State of California to gain the right to operate a booth at the State Fair.

Racially mixed couples are common on the streets of every Northern city and are beginning to appear in the South, and they are far more likely today to be students or professional people than denizens of the underworld. Outlandish costume has become the uniform of youth all over the world who are in moral revolt against a predatory society.

Today, when extra-marital sex is a commonplace, from grammar school to the senior-citizens' clubs, we forget that only a generation ago people were still serving sentences in American prisons for fornication, adultery, and oral sex between men and women, but the police have not forgotten, most of them anyway. A weekly book-review section that once refused advertising of all books whatsoever by Kenneth Patchen or Henry Miller now runs a "cover story" on *The Story of O,* a detailed, graphic description of the most extreme sado-masochism, homosexuality, and "deviance" generally. There are regular underground movie houses which publicly show movies which would shock even a police smoker. Due to their seriousness of intent, they still horrify the police but in a new way.

Adolescent Negro prostitutes in San Francisco when arrested "go limp," and put up long, highly sophisticated arguments for legalized prostitution and do everything but sing *We Shall Overcome.* I must say that the police with whom I have talked who have been involved in such situations have enough sense of humor to think it's all just hilarious.

At one time marihuana and the various pharmaceutical

kicks were part of a hard-dope subculture and unquestionably led in some instances directly to heroin addiction—"Whatsa matter, you chicken? When are you going to graduate?" This is certainly no longer true. The squares and the oldies have no conception of how common the use of marihuana is amongst the young. Pick-up and put-down pills are used by everybody to sleep or wake up and we have just gone through a craze for hallucinogens that seems to be levelling off. It is my impression that this was accompanied by a proportionate decline in the use of heroin except possibly in certain sections of New York City. Although large numbers of informed people believe that marihuana is harmless and that even the worst of the other drugs cause neither delirium tremens, polyneuritis, extensive brain damage nor lung cancer, the police, egged on by some of the press, persist in treating all users of all drugs and intoxicants except alcohol and nicotine as narcotic addicts.

Everybody talks back to the cop today. This "disrespect for law" has two contradictory sources—the general criminality that seeps through all American business and politics, and the growth of a new culture of revolt against precisely this "business ethic." In a sense the police are caught in the middle of a class war, a war between antagonistic moral rather than economic classes.

Most policemen come from conservative levels of the society, lower-middle and working-class families that have preserved an authoritarian structure and fundamentalist religion and puritanical attitude towards sex and a fear and contempt for any nonconformist behavior. The great majority of patrolmen in America have no more than a high-school education and that in substandard schools.

An additional factor seldom taken account of is the class hostility of the people on this social level for the educated, sophisticated, and affluent generally and most especially for those to whom the proper definition of bohemianism specially applies, those who mimic the habits of the idle rich without possessing their money or their reserves of power and who forego the commonly accepted necessities of life to enjoy the luxuries. This type, this model personality, is specifically designed to outrage the type or model policeman who is likely to be suspicious of anybody who drinks brandy instead of bourbon or smokes Turkish cigarettes, much less someone who thinks Juan Marichal must be an obscure Spanish poet.

At one time the great web of police custodial care could isolate such types in Greenwich Village or the Near North Side or North Beach. Today they are everywhere and increasing geometrically. If all of their activities, from peddling poetry on the streets or marching in demonstrations to smoking marihuana and attending nude parties, were suddenly to become accepted, the police forces of the country would be threatened with mass nervous breakdown. This may be one of those processes of historical change where the resistance of the past is not altogether valueless. For instance, laws against the possession of marihuana have become practically unenforceable. If everyone who smoked grass were arrested, we'd have to build concentration camps all over the country. Yet even today it would be quite impossible to legalize marihuana by referendum. It is doubtful if 1 per cent of the state legislators of this country would have the guts to go on record as voting yes on a law like the British one abolishing the criminality of homosexual acts between consenting adults.

The most dangerous social tensions between police and people is certainly in race relations. The most enlightened police chief, with the aid of the most dedicated community-relations detail, cannot control the policeman on the beat, in his personal relations with ignorant, poor, and obstreperous members of a race which he does not understand. The only solution for this within the police force is education and the changing of group pressures. As one police officer said, "We all use the word 'nigger' in the squadroom. You'd be looked on as a kook if you didn't, but I won't let my kids use it at home."

Most chiefs of police rise directly from the ranks and are often less well educated than the new generation of rookies. Most city charters forbid the recruitment of executive officers from outside the force. What this means is that the precinct captains are men from a less enlightened age who have risen by seniority to that point and are not competent to go further.

They are the real bottlenecks and they can defeat all the efforts of an enlightened chief and police commission in their own bailiwicks.

The paramilitary structure of the police force is such that it is exceedingly difficult to create a board of review, or an office of complaints or of human relations within the force which will not be dominated by police politics and civil-service inertia. This is the reason for the ever-growing demand for outside surveillance—civilian policing of the police.

Most cities now have boards of police commissioners of various sorts but these are made up of well-to-do businessmen and politicians and seldom meet more than a couple of hours once a week and have at the best only a small secretarial staff. Negro members are usually lawyers and politicians or pastors of respectable churches. It would be possible totally to reorganize such commissions, make them representative, give them power, and a large working staff.

Within the police force itself it is possible to set up an inspector general's office, outside the chain of command, which would process, investigate, and act on all citizen complaints. This is the common proposal of the more enlightened spokesmen from within the police system.

It would be possible to set up in each city an Ombudsman office with the job of clearing all manner of citizens' dissatisfactions with functioning of the city and its employees. This has worked in Scandinavia from which the word comes, but the vision of pandemonium which the prospect of such an American office conjures up is frightening. It is doubtful if it would be possible to get people to take the jobs and certainly not to stay on them.

A civilian review board, either elected or appointed by the mayor from completely outside all political apparatus, would be ideal but the very terms contain a contradiction. How is this going to come about? It is a popular proposal with the civil-rights organizations and the one most fervently resisted by the police. Although it is true, as Bayard Rustin says, that it would protect the unjustifiably accused officer, it would strip naked the paramilitary structure which the police consider essential, not just to their morale but to their actual function.

In some cities, Seattle and Los Angeles amongst others, the civil-rights organizations have set up civilian patrols who prowl the prowl cars. They follow the police and stand by during arrest, politely and usually silently. They must be made up of citizens of all races, of unimpeachable respectability who are willing to donate eight hours at least once a week to difficult and unpleasant work. Obviously they will obtain from the officers in the patrol cars the most elaborate compliance with all the amenities of the etiquette of arrest. How much effect this has in the long run is questionable and by its nature a civilian patrol program is not likely to endure beyond a few critical months. People are unlikely to engage in such activity night after night, year after year.

What is the best of these alternatives? Only experience can tell. If we were to set up in American cities a kind of neighborhood civil militia which checked on all police activity, we would soon find that we had created a police system like that of the Russians in which the law and the police and their party and neighborhood representatives function as agents of public order and education in social ethics. This may be an estimable theory of how to run a society but it is in total contradiction to every principle of British-American law and social organization. We do not want the police as custodians but as instruments of a law which regards all men as equal and at liberty to run their affairs to suit themselves as long as they do not inflict damage on others.

The police spokesmen are perfectly right in saying that what should be done is truly to professionalize police work. This means changing the class foundation of the police force itself. A professional is a man with a salary at least comparable to that of a small-town dentist, with at least one college degree, with an advanced technical and at the same time broadly humanistic education and whose work demands that he keep abreast of its latest developments. The thought of turning all the policemen in America into such persons staggers the imagination. However, the nursing profession, which by and large is recruited from exactly the same level of society as the police, has been professionalized in one generation in everything but salary. An executive nurse in a big-city health department may have more years of college than most of the doctors working with her. She is lucky indeed if she makes $800 a month.

What is the answer? I have no idea. This is one of those many regions of frustration which are spreading across all of modern life, blotches on the skin of a body which is sick within with a sickness of which all diagnoses differ. I suppose society will smell its way to some sort of solution, muddle through the muddle. This is not a very hopeful prognostication for what is, after all, one aspect of a grave crisis, but none of the other prognostications about any of the other aspects is hopeful either.

TOM SAWYER IN TROUBLE

A bearded Tom Sawyer, nattily clad in a policeman's tunic and blue jeans, had a run-in with authority here yesterday.

Unlike his Mark Twain namesake, San Francisco's Sawyer lost this round to a pair of policemen.

Officers Tony Delzompo and Jim Bailey, in fact, found the wearing of parts of police uniforms so unamusing they arrested Sawyer.

Sawyer, 23, of 1253 Willard Street in the Haight-Ashbury district, was booked on suspicion of possession of stolen property.

The officers admitted that there was no report of stolen police jackets on file, but said that Sawyer's uniform, nonetheless, might well be stolen.

Sawyer, questioned at 7 P.M. at Frederick and Stanyan streets by the officers, told them he got the jacket from a friend.

Perhaps an explanation for the officers' investigative zeal could be found in Sawyer's substitute for the police badge, a large lapel button pinned on the left side of the tunic. It read:

"Overthrow the Government."

—*San Francisco Chronicle,* August 22, 1966

Note: When this article appeared in "Playboy" they say the Boss Heat in San Francisco got me fired from three jobs at once, one of which I had held for almost ten years. Can I prove it? No. My informants "refuse to testify." 1967.

10. The Second Post-War, the Second Interbellum, the Permanent War Generation

I.

In the winter of 1954–55 America was in an economic, social, and cultural interregnum. One style of life, one mood—like Victorianism or Edwardianism—was giving way to another. The industrial age based on the mechanical exploitation of coal and iron was giving way to electronics, computers, automation—with all the social and intellectual results such a basic revolution implies—but as yet few indeed understood what was happening. The country was in a minor economic depression following the end of the Korean War. The Korean War represented a qualitative leap forward in technology and a lag in all other factors. However, morale broke down for a more simple reason. You can fight only one such war every twenty-five years. The Korean War took place within the effective memory of the Second World War. The academic and intellectual establishment, Left, Right, and Center, was shattered, demoralized, and discredited by the years of McCarthyism. Young men by the thousands were returning from the Korean War to the colleges disillusioned and contemptuous of their elders. They said to each other, "Keep your nose clean and don't volunteer." "Don't believe anybody over thirty." Communication between groups broke down. Only those of the older generation who had remained defiant were respected, listened to, questioned. Just as the Army took years to discover the almost total breakdown of morale in Korea, so the older intellectuals were unaware that a volcano was building up under them.

McCarthyism itself was an expression of breakdown of an older American synthesis. It has often been pointed out that McCarthy came from a small Wisconsin city, from a state which was once the home of the radical Progressive LaFollette, the most intransigent spokesman for the old agrarian Populism with its distrust of Wall Street, the New York and New England political and cultural establishment, isolationist, defiantly middle class. The doors were closed and locked forever for any escape into economic power of the Midwestern debtor society of small farmers, small-town independent merchants, and country bankers. McCarthyism is the last expression of what in central Europe was called the Green Revolution, devouring itself in impotence.

Most of the slogans of McCarthyism, like those of the John Birch Society today, had once possessed an entirely different meaning and had been formative ideas in the shaping of an older America. This content had been emptied out and replaced by truculent suspicion of any and all enlightened ideas which were forming the new, succeeding society. At the top America was in the hands of a sort of regency. The ship of state was steering itself. A generation was growing up which had known World War II only as children. Not one of the hopes or the promises of that war had been realized. Russia and the United States both had the Bomb and were striving to divide the world between them, to turn whole nations into aircraft carriers and army bases. The Korean War had ended in a bloody stalemate and a wholesale breakdown of morale. While McCarthy was at the height of his power, with few exceptions the intellectual and moral leaders of America feared to challenge, if they did not actually support him. The entire academic community was shattered and terrorized both by McCarthy and dozens of local witch hunts and state-sponsored investigating committees. McCarthyism more than any other thing revealed to the young the moral bankruptcy of their elders. College professors complained that they were facing a silent generation who received their lectures with the response "no comment." Nihilism in public life was reflected in nihilism amongst young intellectuals. The intellectual establishment, in fact, many of whom were ex-Communists, largely supported McCarthy. Nihilism in authority breeds nihilism in response, as it did in nineteenth-century Russia.

Although all the literary editors and the academicians were busy telling the world in the early Fifties that the age of experiment and revolt was over, a very few critics, myself amongst them, had begun to point out that this slogan alone showed how complete was the breakdown of communications between the generations. Under the very eyes of the pre-war generation a new age of experiment and revolt far more drastic in its departures, far more absolute in its rejections, was already coming into being. The Beat writers were not at first part of this movement. Kerouac had published a very conventional novel, Ginsberg was writing dry whimsical little imitations of William Carlos Williams, Burroughs' intoxicated lucubrations were not considered publishable even by himself. Gregory Corso, a naïve writer, a kind of natural-born Dadaist, was tolerated as an amusing mascot by the boys on *The Harvard Advocate* as a convenient practical joke.

San Francisco was the one community in the United States which had a regional literature and art at variance with the prevailing pattern. During the Thirties it had become a strong trade-union town with a politically powerful Left, yet this radical activity was remarkably independent of the doctrinnaire dictates of the American Communist Party. Perhaps the main reason for this was that most of the leadership had come from the I.W.W., the Anarcho-Syndicalist "One Big Union" movement which had been so strong on the Pacific Coast a generation before. During the war, work camps for conscientious objectors were established throughout the mountains and forests of California. These boys came down to San Francisco on their leaves. They met with San Francisco writers and artists who had been active in the Red Thirties but who had become, not professional anti-Bolsheviks, but anarchists and pacifists. During the war, meetings of pacifist and anarchist organizations continued to be well attended. Immediately on the war's end a group of San Francisco writers and artists began an Anarchist Circle with public meetings which for five years were better attended than those of all the Socialist and Communist organizations put together. From this group and from the artists' C.O. camp at Waldport, Oregon, came a large percentage of cultured activities in San Francisco which have lasted to the present time—a radio station, three little theaters, a succession of magazines, and a number of people who are considered the leading writers and artists of the community today. And it was this sympathetic environment that the so-called Beat writers discovered around the early Fifties.

There is probably more misunderstanding and misinformation current about the Beat Generation than any other phenomenon in contemporary culture. This is due to the fact that the sensational press were quick to seize on the Beat writers and to reconstruct them in their own image. The public personality which had been grafted onto Allen Ginsberg is the kind of person the editors of *Time* magazine would be if they only had the nerve. The Beat writer is what the French call a *hallucination publicitaire,* Madison Avenue's idea of a Revolutionary Bohemian Artist. It bears almost no relation to actuality although the delusion, the false image, is a continuous temptation to the real writers. They can always find applause and profit by living up to the delusions of their enemies. The factual historical misinformation about the Beat Movement is immense. In the first place, there never really was a Beat Movement, with the exception of four writers—Allen Ginsberg, Jack Kerouac, William Burroughs, and Gregory Corso. Second, these writers have had little connection with San Francisco down the years and they were all fairly well known amongst bohemian intellectuals before they ever saw the city. William Burroughs, several years older than the rest, had first brought them together in New York shortly after 1950. Kerouac and Ginsberg were at that time students at Columbia and Gregory

Corso a non-student at Harvard University. For several years a group of very hip young men had been running a magazine in St. Louis called *Neurotica.* About 1952 two of the editors, Jay and Fred Landesman, moved to New York and opened a large loft studio a block away from the San Remo Café, then the most in or the most far out of the Greenwich Village bohemian hangouts. It was at the Landesmans' studio that Kerouac, Ginsberg, Corso, and Burroughs first made contact with the literary bohemian society of New York. There are several novels about this phase of the movement. With the exception of Clellan Holmes's *Go,* they very significantly do not concentrate on the specific behavior patterns peculiar to the four Beats but describe the general scene in the first post-war generation of disaffiliation, revolt, disgust.

The trouble with the New York scene around the San Remo Café was its total mindlessness. There was nothing there but disgust. When Ginsberg and Kerouac began visiting San Francisco in the course of their student wanderings around the country during vacation the effect on them was explosive. In 1956 I asked the proprietors of the Six Gallery, one of the launching pads of abstract expressionism, if they would sponsor a reading by Walter Lowenfels who could not get a hall anywhere in San Francisco because he was under indictment for violation of the Smith Act. He was an editor of the Philadelphia edition of *The Daily Worker* and had been a well-known modernist poet in the Paris America of the late Twenties and early Thirties. (He is the Jabberwohl Kronstadt in Henry Miller's *Black Spring.*) The proprietors of the gallery were delighted at the chance to defy authority. Nobody under 40 had ever heard of Lowenfels as a poet but to everyone's amazement the large gallery was jam-packed with young people who came to hear him read. The proprietors were so delighted that they asked me to arrange other readings. The next one made history. It was a parade of the city's leading avant-garde poets—Robert Duncan, Brother Antoninus, Philip Lamantia, Lawrence Ferlinghetti, Michael McClure, and four young men who had just come to town—Gary Snyder, Philip Whalen, Gregory Corso, Allen Ginsberg. Here Ginsberg first read *Howl* which he had been working on in a state of excited entrancement for the past two weeks. The effect beggars description. A new folklore and a new folkloristic relationship between audience and poet had been created.

The Six Gallery reading is usually said to have launched the Beat movement. In fact the only connection is Allen Ginsberg himself. Kerouac was present but did not participate except to create periodic disturbances. Public reading of poetry had become a regular institution in San Francisco as early as 1928 and was a principal attraction in the John Reed Club, the Communist artist and writers' organization, and in the Jack London Club, the competing Socialist group. Poetry readings were given by the united pacifist Randolph Bourne Council and later by the San Francisco Anarchist Circle all through the war and the decade after, mostly in the Arbeiter Ring, the largely Jewish workingmen's fraternal organization. The San Francisco Poetry Center had been in existence for some years and had already moved to San Francisco State College. The annual Poetry Festivals had begun shortly after the war and the satirical musical review, *The Poets' Follies,* under the direction of Weldon Kees and Michael Grieg, with acts like the beautiful stripper Lili St. Cyr reading T. S. Eliot's *Ash Wednesday* (dressed), had already shown three consecutive years. Kenneth Patchen, Lawrence Ferlinghetti, and myself had already started reading poetry to jazz in local jazz clubs. (The great bassist and composer Charles Mingus was closely associated with many of the artists and writers of San Francisco during the war years.)

The older poets had all been active in the anarchist and pacifist movement for many years, had been conscientious objectors during the war, and worked in C.O. camps or in hospitals. Of the younger, Philip Whalen and Gary Snyder had grown up in I.W.W. circles in Oregon and Washington.

It was from this background that the very superficial and largely factitious interest in Zen Buddhism shared by Kerouac and Ginsberg comes, not, as is often imagined, from contact with G.I.'s returning from China, Japan, and Korea. The influence of Oriental religion on San Francisco is partly indigenous. There are many large, flourishing Buddhist churches in the Bay Area with mostly Japanese congregations, but with Caucasians as well, and with many contacts with the general community. I know of only one returned G.I. who came back with an interest in Buddhism. He had no contact with the San Francisco intellectual community except myself and became an academic Buddhologist. On the other hand, Alan Watts, Gerald Heard, Christopher Isherwood, Aldous Huxley, and myself in California and the painters Mark Tobey and Morris Graves in Seattle were centers of interest in Oriental religion, but more especially in the revival of the contemplative life, all through the war years. Most of us conducted seminars, discussion groups, and retreats teaching younger people the elements and the techniques of nonviolence and meditation. These activities of course still go on in different forms and on a much larger scale. Gary Snyder is an ordained Zen monk and learned in the poetry and religious literature of India, China, and Japan. I will always remember the night Jack Kerouac appeared uninvited at my home, sat down with a jug of cheap port wine beside him on the floor, announced that he was a Zen Buddhist, and discovered that everybody in the room read at least one Oriental language.

Kerouac's portrayal of this aspect of San Francisco culture, in *The Dharma Bums,* would be a malevolent libel if it were deliberate. It is only an expression of his own baffled ignorance in the face of human motivations and beliefs, which he was intrinsically incapable of understanding. It is this ignorant confabulation presenting itself as reality which accounts for the almost complete eclipse of Kerouac's reputation. Young people no longer read him and consider him absurd, the apotheosis of uptight. It is not just the misrepresentation of fact but the misunderstanding of motivation, the distortion of character and the ignorance of the ideas involved which has caused him to be no longer read by people who really understand what he is talking about. The world view of post-modern culture and of the San Francisco version of it especially has now become the common possession of millions of young people and it is backed up with a whole literature and way of life which bears no real resemblance to the disorderly conduct for its own sake of Kerouac's characters.

Another influence on the San Francisco scene was Henry

Miller who had lived in Big Sur since 1941 and who was known to most of the San Francisco writers. I doubt if either Ginsberg or Kerouac ever read much of what he has written. They once hitchhiked down the coast 130 miles to visit him and were not admitted. Miller's very positive and powerful religious convictions and love of life have little to do with the nihilism of the beatnik.

I should mention by the way that the world "beatnik" was invented by the San Francisco columnist, Herb Caen. The term "beat" was a common slang phrase amongst bop musicians and often, like "funky," and other bop slang, was used in a reverse sense, but usually to mean emotionally exhausted. The term "Beat Generation" was first used simultaneously by Clellan Holmes, in an article in the *New York Times Magazine,* and by myself in *New World Writing.* This article and others like it which I wrote at the time about the then youngest generation of poets—the new age of experiment and revolt—included along with Ginsberg and Corso, Charles Olson, Robert Creeley, Denise Levertov, Lawrence Ferlinghetti, Robert Duncan, Brother Antoninus, and many others. This was an unfortunate linkage which has endured to this day. None of these people has anything to do with any imagined Beat movement. Their writing is of the widest variety and they share only a rejection of the morals of a commercial civilization and a return to the international idiom of modern verse which had been stifled in America by the Reactionary Generation of the Forties and the proletarians of the Thirties.

William Carlos Williams and Ezra Pound, but Williams especially, were strong influences on this entire group, as were the unreconstructed modernists surviving from the interbellum years —Louis Zukofsky, Walter Lowenfels, Sam Beckett, Kenneth Patchen, and myself. Another factor in San Francisco culture that is very important is its closer connection with London and Paris than with New York. San Francisco intellectuals first made contact with London Anarchists during the Spanish War and all during the Second World War correspondence was kept up with people like Sir Herbert Read, Alex Comfort, George Woodcock, Charles Wrey Gardner, Tambimuttu, and others. I for instance first read the poetry of Denise Levertov when she was a Land

Girl in Essex and introduced her by mail to Charles Wrey Gardner who was publishing *Poetry Quarterly* in Billericay. George Barker lived in Big Sur in the Forties. Dylan Thomas spent two long periods in San Francisco.

French publications of the *résistance* like *Editions de minuit* and Pierre Seghers' *Poesie* arrived in G.I. mail in some quantity as soon as the Americans got to Africa, and lesser amounts had trickled in from the very beginning. Writers like Simone Weil, Sartre, Camus, and poets of the *résistance* like Char, Frenaud, Rousselot, Seghers, Follain, Guillevic, were read in San Francisco before anyone in New York literary circles had so much as heard of them. People in San Francisco had corresponded with Simone Weil from the days of the Spanish War.

All this goes to make up the picture of the emergence of the post-modern worldwide intellectual culture in which the Beat Generation was only a minor episode, a kind of misunderstanding on the part of a few intellectual amateurs and following them the literary journalists of the gutter press. The present revolt of youth, the new radicalism, the democratization of the avant-garde, are all aspects of a worldwide revolution in the very foundations of culture, basic changes in ways of living, the emergence of a fundamentally new civilization. Allen Ginsberg has survived into this new civilization, and is today one of its leading figures in Tel Aviv, Calcutta, Moscow, but the Beat Generation placard which was hung around his neck has long since dropped away. Only squares and elderly Communist bureaucrats in the minor Balkan countries used the term "beatnik" after 1960.

What was the significance of the Beat movement, so called? What was its effect on the evolution of American literature and culture? It was the form in which the mass disaffiliation of post-war youth from a commercial, predatory, and murderous society first came to the attention of that society itself. Kerouac's *On the Road* was a bestseller. It served the purpose of detective stories and cowboy romances and girlie magazines for the vast new white-collar class, the grey flannel suburbia escaped into a dream world of fast cars, easy women, drunken parties.

This world of Jack Kerouac's had essentially the same values as did the world of the upwardly mobile new professions. A whole literature of dope, homosexual prostitution, knife fights, sado-masochism, gang bangs has followed in its train—the soap operas and horse operas of the lumpen petty power élite, the little Jet or Squirt Set, in the decade since its publication. Their life has gradually come to resemble their escape literature. The effect of Kerouac on young people, on the revolt of youth, on the genuinely disaffiliated, was minimal. True, all sorts of juvenile delinquents abandoned their disorderly conduct in the soda fountains near the high schools of Cle Elum, Fort Dodge, and Tucumcari, hitchhiked to San Francisco, and started making like Kerouac's characters in North Beach. But this invasion vanished like the Gauls from Rome. It was unable to hold the territory. While it lasted it had certain characteristics that distinguished it from the older bohemia or the present worldwide culture of secession. It was life-denying. It hated sex. It used alcohol only for oblivion. One of the diagnostic signs of the Beat syndrome, very obvious in Kerouac's and Burroughs' books, was contempt for women. The Beat come-on was to treat a girl exactly as one would treat a casual homosexual pickup in a public convenience. An interesting thing about the winter of 1957 in North Beach was the wave of young girl suicides, one of them the mistress of the hero of *On the Road*. Another man had killed his wife in Mexico some years before, playing William Tell at a party. This kind of senseless nihilism was pushed aside by the rising tide of genuine revolt with a new ethic and a new kind of social responsibility and a new and very male and very female sexuality—even though the squares are still bothered because everybody wears long hair.

Burroughs is a special case. His work is source material for social history, not literature, and as such of minor importance. He is also one of many writers mining a current fadism. Corso is another special case. Like most naïves, he really has little relationship to literary literature. It is possible to relate *le douanier* Rousseau to the beginnings of Cubism but the relationship is fortuitous. If anything, they were influenced by him, certainly not the other way around. He wanted to paint as photographically as possible. This does not mean that Corso is not a considerable poet; he is, just as Rousseau is a very great painter.

Of the four Beat writers, Ginsberg is much the most important. *Howl* has sold hundreds of thousands of copies and been translated into most civilized languages and many semi-civilized ones. It is a true vatic utterance, the speech of a *nabi,* an excited Hebrew prophet, and the closest parallels in literature are Hosea and Jeremiah. For several years it was fantastically popular with American students and played an important role in re-enforcing and consolidating their contempt for the conspiracy of the Social Lie—the American Way of Life. Ginsberg has none of the life hatred, nihilism, praise for oblivion, sexual disgust, or social destructiveness of Kerouac and Burroughs. He has never lost a certain boyish ingenuousness which leads him to showing off on television and provoking arguments about dope and homosexuality with Bolshevik bureaucrats. In some ways he resembles, most especially in his unquenchable youthfulness, Colin Wilson. The great difference between the Angries and the Beats is that the Americans rejected the entire social structure. They didn't want to be admitted to the old Establishment or to found a new one. They wanted to pull down all Establishments whatsoever. More important even than this—all of them, even Kerouac and Burroughs, were interested in what the avant-garde between the wars called The Revolution of the Word. They were interested in attacking, disorganizing, and in the case of Ginsberg and Corso, reorganizing the structure of the human sensibility as such through a revolutionary use of language, the overturning of the old patterns of logic and syntax. This last phrase is almost exactly that of the surrealist theoretician André Breton and it is still believed in passionately by the Beat poets. On the other hand, I have found in interviews with the leading Angries that when you question them about this matter they are unable to understand what you are talking about—it's some French thing, like eating frogs and snails. An American television interviewer, after a long hassle trying to get the most articulate of the Angries to understand what he was talking about, gave up with the remark, aired throughout the world, "I guess I'd be angry too if I went to all that trouble and ended up writing like bum Galsworthy." Whatever the faults of the Beats, they were the first challenge to what we call the basic values of the civilization to reach a popular audience, but it must be remembered that they were essentially a small focal point in an overwhelming social movement, a highly visible ripple in a worldwide New Wave.

II.

The most significant, if not the best by older critical standards, literature in America today is to be found, not in books, or even in the established literary magazines, but in poetry readings, in mimeographed broadsides, in lyrics for rock groups, in protest songs—in direct audience relationships of the sort that prevailed at the very beginnings of literature. The art of reading and writing could vanish from memory in a night and it would not make a great difference to the poetry, or even much of the prose, of the youngest generation of poets and hearers of poetry. This is the new world of youth which so disturbs the oldies. Rightly so, it is a world they never made. In it they are strangers and afraid—totally unable, most of them, to comprehend what is happening.

The last few years have seen a steady stream of American books on the New Left, on the revolt of youth, and especially on such mass phenomena as the Free Speech Movement in Berkeley and the anti-Vietnam protests on all the campuses. With no exceptions these books have been written by ideologues, men of the Thirties, or by somewhat younger people who grew up in lingering Marxist sectarian groups. They all try to assimilate a non-ideological, non-political worldwide movement to the programmatic delusions of another age.

What we are witnessing today is a profound change in the patterns of life and an even greater change in its possibilities. This affects all nations—I used to say except Red China—beatniks, hooligans, *gammlers, stilyagi,* provos, hippies—they're not just to be found in Amsterdam, in the East Village in New York, on Haight Street in San Francisco, or on Notting Hill in London. Terms of abuse only represent the attempt of the squares and the oldies to exorcise behavior which they do not understand with stereotyped formulas which they think they do.

Britain is a special case. British society assimilates all things —the ceremonies of the monarchy, the country house orgies of high life, the stodgy Communist Party of Great Britain. Today the Teddy Boys are middle-aged; the Angries lunch in the Reform Club; and even Mods and Rockers, no longer young, have been digested by a homogeneous and homogenizing society. Carnaby Street is already part of the Establishment and a tourist attraction second only to the boys in bearskin busbys. The subculture of secession in Great Britain is a kind of Fabian anarchism, slowly penetrating all structures of the society by metastasis. This is not true anywhere else and it makes the profound and ever-widening schism in the soul in modern society difficult to explain to a British audience. Can you imagine an American president making the very influential American anarchist, critic, poet, psychiatrist, urbanist, educator, Paul Goodman, a knight like Sir Herbert Read, or Bob Dylan an M.B.E. like John Lennon?

Most nations show no capacity to absorb their youth culture. Not only does the sight of the long coiffure give most premiers, ministers, and cabinet secretaries running and barking fits, but it is becoming increasingly difficult for young people in the uniform of secession—beards, long hair, blue jeans—to cross national boundaries. They are harassed with elaborate customs inspections and forced to give proof of their solvency and in some countries, Greece, Morocco, and Algiers for instance, are refused entrance on their appearance alone. *Les douaniers* are perfectly right; they are the enemy. If there were enough of them national boundaries would disappear instantly.

Does this mean that they are Internationalists and Pacifists, capital I and capital P? Certainly not. Any question like this provokes a false answer. What is happening cannot be explained in terms of ideology. Ideologies are at best schematizations of social reality, never fit the facts, and wear out rapidly like ill-fitting shoes. Suppose Hitler had conquered the world and had totally suppressed all the documents and the very memory of the writings of Marx. Would the industrial process then have failed to produce "human self-alienation"? Would there no longer be any necessity for the capitalist system to expand regardless of human values or else collapse? Would the ratio of labor power to capital investment and with it the rate of profit stop falling? Would the failure of the economic system to insure a minimum of life satisfactions for the majority of its members not have resulted in an ever-increasing demand for a fundamental change in the quality of life? Do all these things depend upon familiarity with a four-foot shelf of books full of errors and failed prophecies? Revolutionary consciousness is not the product of courses in the ABC of Marxism. It is a kind of natural secretion of the hopeless contradictions of modern society and it is most doubtful if Marx would have recognized it —in fact he notoriously was as intolerant as any country pastor in Ibsen of the mild bohemianism of his own children.

Fortunately for the present generation, the hundred years from 1848 to 1948 witnessed the total bankruptcy of all ideologies. The revolutions of the past, said Teilhard de Chardin, had economic and political objectives, but the latter half of the twentieth century will see a worldwide revolutionary struggle to change the quality and meaning of life. This revolution cannot be understood unless we realize that it starts off with the slate wiped clean. There is no worse guide conceivable than an aged ex-Left-Trotskyite holding down a professorship in a multiversity, the boss of a corps of graduate students tagging demonstrators about the campus with questionnaires.

Today there is growing up throughout the world an entirely new pattern of life. For several years I have called it the subculture of secession but this it is no more—it is a competing civilization. "a new society within the shell of the old." It has come about not through books or programs but through a change in the methods of production. It is a society of people who have simply walked into a computerized, transistorized, automated world, a post-industrial or post-capitalist economy, in which there is an ever-increasing democratization of at least the possibilities for a creative response to life.

What does democratization of the arts mean in practice in America? What happens when an entire subculture takes to poetry, rock groups, folk songs, junk sculpture, collage pop pictures, total sexual freedom, and costumes invented *ad lib?* What is the relationship of this literary and artistic activity in which everyone can take part to the official, professionalized culture? What is the relationship of the Establishment and the Secession?

Obviously the younger people are both seceding from something and acceding to something. What?

Conventional academic poetry is certainly flourishing in America. Most poets of this type, in fact all of them, have very good jobs in universities which pay from $8,000 to $30,000 a year. Their books do not sell, but readings on the poetry circuits of the Establishment are at least as profitable as ever was Vaudeville. Any established poet can ask and receive fees from $500 to $1,000 an appearance, thus nuzzling the heels of concert stars on the rung above him.

There is another world of poetry readings altogether. Ferlinghetti, Ginsberg, and Bob Dylan form the only bridge from one world to another. I have no idea what Bob Dylan's sales are, but Ferlinghetti's *Coney Island of the Mind* alone had sold 250,000 copies by 1969. The book sells at the rate of 45,000 a year and has been translated into Swedish, Danish, Polish, Russian, French, Italian, German, Spanish, Czech, Slovak, Serbian, at least, not counting pirated editions in the Orient and in the smaller Iron Curtain countries. Ferlinghetti's other books sell 20,000 a year, altogether. Ginsberg's *Howl* has sold over 200,000 in the U.S. alone. *Kaddish* had sold 30,000. *Reality Sandwiches*, 20,000. The foreign editions of Ginsberg are innumerable. Dylan Thomas's sales are still about equal to Ginsberg's or Ferlinghetti's and he was one of the most popular "platform personalities" in American history—but not in Great Britain!

People like Bob Dylan, Joan Baez, and the leading rock groups have fabulous incomes. Yet even those who have gone over to the nightclub circuit like Peter, Paul, and Mary and Judy Collins still live essentially the same lives as the seceders on unemployment payments or welfare with the same values and the same pleasures, and they are even more active in civil-rights and civil-liberties struggles. That is the point—in a society of abundance where the poor live better than Charlemagne, everybody can afford to be ethical. Aristotle confines his *Nichomachean Ethics* to the moral behavior of free citizens of Greek city states. Slaves, says he, cannot afford ethics—their wills are not their own. The reason for the vast eruption of moral protest in America since the beginning of the civil-rights struggle is that people now can afford to be good—aggressively so. Nothing serious, except possibly murder, can happen to a young girl who leaves a Northern college and goes to the South to help out. Suppose her parents disown her? She won't starve. She'll have an interesting life and be welcomed back to school with a scholarship. In an abundant society a large number of people will discover that ethics is (or are) fun—like poetry or jazz or happenings. Only in a wealthy society could the film play so important a role. Kenneth Anger, Stan Brakage, Bruce Conner, James Broughton, one of their films costs more than James Joyce made on *Ulysses*—yet these film-makers are as much a part of the scene as Gary Snyder, whose life motto is, "Don't own anything you wouldn't leave out in the rain"—or as Joan Baez, who must make as much as Maria Callas.

Far more important than their large sales, readings by Ginsberg, Ferlinghetti, Gary Snyder are mass demonstrations where the charisma practically reeks, and could be bottled and sold. In the new subculture, no longer very submerged, these poets have founded a way of life. In countless coffee shops and community pads people gather nightly, play records of rock groups like The Jefferson Airplane, The Grateful Dead, The Only Alternative and the Other Possibilities, records of protest and of folk singers like Bob Dylan and Joan Baez, or records of the modern jazz musicians, Ornette Coleman, John Handy, Cecil Taylor, Archie Shepp; or they may beat congas and atonal guitars polyrhythmically and recite their own poetry. Usually this poetry has no life beyond the immediate occasion. Sometimes small groups, essentially neighborhood communities, in the analogs of New York's East Village and San Francisco's Haight-Ashbury district, which are springing up all over the country, get together and put out duplicated publications of their own poems. Sometimes they even manage a hand press, and produce a regular magazine. The girls set type, the fellows turn the cranks, babies crawl on the floor, and cats tip over the fonts and piss in the pied type. The first magazine of this kind from such a group was *The Ark,* published just after World War II by the San Francisco Anarchist Circle. Since 1946 its progeny are numbered in thousands, but they still come from the same kind of group (although nobody is so square as to call himself an anarchist anymore), and are produced in the same circumstances in the same cold water flats with rubbish décor.

Like the old French Canadian threat of winning the battle of the cradle, this is a revolution which hopes to win simply by outliving and outbreeding the squares. In a few years most people will be under 25. In this world there are no economic problems. This is the world of post-Theobald man, functioning on the bare minimum subsistence income which the modern Welfare State actually does guarantee right now. These people not only accept their redundancy, they glory in it. Nobody works any more than enough to get his unemployment insurance. The standard of living is exactly that of the unsophisticated redundants—two pairs of blue jeans a year in Appalachian fashion, welfare cuisine of lots of rice and beans, wine at $1.30 a gallon, and grass consumed till every roach has vanished from its crutch. Where the records and books come from, I don't know. I guess they're stolen. Paintings, and found art, like the poetry, are authentic products of cottage industry.

If you democratize art you necessarily, at least at first, lower its standards. Anybody can do junk sculpture or drip painting or collages. Anybody can sing as well as Bob Dylan. Anybody can write as well as most of the poems given away in San Francisco shops by the Free Poetry Movement (on the butcher's counter a stack of mimeographed sheets and a card, "Free Poems—Take One"). When Lenin said the time would come when any cook could run the State he didn't say he'd be a very good cook or a very good governor. However, already a new set of artistic and literary values or criteria are emerging. They reflect the interpersonal relationships and their attendant values of a quite different kind of society—anti-predatory, anti-exploitative, personally, morally engaged. This results in a quite different formal esthetic—and through all the apparent chaos, a new concept of form can be seen emerging and new evaluations. Fifty years of socialist power have not ended human self-alienation but seem to have increased it. You can't expect the Free Poetry Movement to produce Homers overnight or even T. S. Eliots. However—the Seceders have attacked precisely alienation and I suppose that is the fundamental criterion: does this poem or song or story or film or painting or play overcome the gulf between man and man and between man and himself—even a very little?

This is a revolutionary movement which has substituted for "Workers of the World Unite—You Have Nothing to Lose But Your Chains," "Please Let Me Alone, Man; I Just Want to Do Nice Things With My Friends." Innocuous as this might seem as a revolutionary slogan, it is a spectre that is haunting Europe, and America, and Asia as well. In Prague there was a coffee-shop called "The Viola" where Ferlinghetti was recited to records by Thelonius Monk, although in Prague in *cette belle époque* between the wars nobody ever thought to recite Allen Tate to Stephen Foster on the banjo.

Poetry, probably because it is the one art most difficult to turn into a commodity, is, with folk-rock and jazz, the focus of life in this world. An equally important reason is that contemporary disaffiliation is essentially a religious challenge to the universal hypocrisy of the Social Lie, and poetry, of all the arts, can give most specific, most overt, most challenging expression to religious values. Beginning with *Howl,* which is a poem by a *nabi* of the New York Subway, strictly in Allen Ginsberg's own tradition, that of the Hebrew prophets, most of the poetry of the subculture of secession has been religious and its practitioners have been devoted to the theological virtues—voluntary poverty, sexual honesty, and obedience to personal integrity.

In such a culture, particularly if it is floated by, rather than submerged in, an affluent society like our own, economic questions wither away, more rapidly than in Lenin's State. The significant poetry of the youngest generation escapes altogether from the strictures of the dismal science. These are the people who have walked into the Great Society uninvited, without even turning down an invitation to The White House. They have taken possession of the social results of the cybernetic future.

Political organizations that represent one pole or the other of the vast evil try to use this subculture without success. Turnouts like the great Vietnam protests are not organized by the Progressive Labor Party or the Students for a Democratic Society or any of the other tiny neo-Bolshevik groups that crowd their way into the TV cameras. They crank out leaflets and go through the mechanical patterns of "leading the struggle" but they are very minor external parasites on the tail of a vast mass movement. When they take over and force their people to the front, they find themselves without followers. The youth of America—or the rest of the world for that matter—do not protest the Vietnam War for geopolitical reasons, in the interests of Chairman Mao or Ho Chi Minh or the Kremlin—but as a murderous conspiracy of the aged, and for purely human and moral reasons. They look on the war as a war of the old men at the desks and on the podiums against the young men and women in the rice paddies and behind the guns. When political groups try to force this protest into their own channels they discover that the protestors have suddenly gone away. The crazier violent groups are doubtless, as always, 75 per cent *agents provocateurs.*

There is a good deal of confusion about several quite different types of youth behavior. Just because conduct is revolting, that doesn't mean it is revolt. There is no more relationship between the wild boys of the road—motorcycle clubs like Hell's Angels or some of the more violent Rocker types—and poets like Gary Snyder or singers like Bob Dylan or Joan Baez, than there is between an Establishment writer like John Osborne and people who hunt foxes. A good part of what goes on amongst people under thirty is simply the perennial youth culture we have always had, which has always disturbed the old, from Babylon to Benny Goodman. Today the opportunities for mischief offered by affluent society simply make it all that more conspicuous.

When the Hell's Angels announced they were going to disrupt the Vietnam protest march in Berkeley, Ken Kesey and Allen Ginsberg invited the leaders down to Kesey's mountain home and turned them on with LSD and the next day they were as meek as lambs, loved all sentient creatures, and rode in the march on Kesey's Op-Art truck. That's the connection.

Which brings up the subject of narcotics. It is true that more young people smoke marihuana than drink alcohol (except for wine and beer). They say it is obviously less harmful, and less harmful than tobacco. Most medical opinion agrees with them. The reason for the persecution by the State is that marihuana is impossible to tax. Anybody can grow it in a window box in a moderately dry and warm climate. But by very definition, a pleasure which is not taxable is a vice.

As for LSD and the various hallucinogens and stimulants (speed)—the more dangerous ones are losing their popularity. People who use LSD claim that it doesn't cause lung cancer or lead men to beat their wives or women to let their children starve. Since older Americans smoke two to four packs of lethal cigarettes a day and consume immense quantities of alcohol—solely to get drunk—and go to sleep with the goof ball and get up with a pep pill—their moral horror when they discover their children smoke grass or drop acid is a little disgusting. I have been in some pretty low pads but I have never been in one whose atmosphere of evil and debauchery approached by miles that of an ordinary financial district junior executives' and stenographers' cocktail bar.

Total sexual freedom—astonishingly enough to the elders—doesn't seem to make a great deal of difference. There is total sexual freedom in the Wall Street or Madison Avenue cocktail lounge too—but there it is motivated by malevolent mutual hostility and exploitation. In the typical post-Beat cooperative rooming house it is usually motivated by a rather excessively aggressive mutual affection, a vulgarized hobo Buddhism. An older-type square is liable to turn off abruptly when the young lady poet says as she takes him to bed, "I just love all sentient creatures, don't you, hunh?" Most remarkable is the sharp decline in homosexuality in a completely permissive environment.

Again, the Carnaby Street costume is often confused with the Revolt of Youth. This is absurd. Carnaby Street is for the rich—rich by the standards of the secession. It is a remarkably successful attempt of London to disrupt and capture some of the international fashion trade so long held by Paris and then by Italy and New York. (The Beatles and Carnaby Street are what defunct empires produce, attempting to rectify the balance of payments when everybody can make their own steel.) Nor is it really peculiarly British. Clothes like this are common now everywhere amongst the junior Jet or Squirt Set. Portobello Road and Waterlooplein costumes—Edwardian evening gowns topped by 1840 army dress tunics, or togas, or chitons worn with high button boots are something else. This fashion for optional dress —dress any way you want—began in San Francisco and New York about 1960. Before that it had been confined to a small handful of post-Beat intellectuals and their girls, mostly in San Francisco—but with a few friends in the East Village. Now it is also worldwide but I think it is more than a fashion—it is here to stay. In the future probably both rich and poor will dress anyway they like. The society can produce an unlimited variety of costume. Clothes are certainly not crucial—but it is beards, long hair, bare feet, that seem to distress the oldies more than even dope and promiscuity.

What lies back of all this confusion is simply that the older generation believes that those who reject their values *must* be delinquents. They are incapable of seeing that a new culture with a new system of values has sprung up around them. People ask loaded questions like: Do they sponge on their parents for a college education? No. In the American West a college education costs so little it can be earned by part-time work. Many students attend classes without registering or paying anything and the hipper teachers wink at them. I conducted a seminar last year in which half the students, and by far the better half, were so called non-students.

Do they loaf and write poetry on welfare or unemployment payments—in other words on the taxpayers' money? What's wrong with that? Better write poetry with the taxes than what any current administration is doing with them. One bomber destroyed while attacking a bamboo bridge or burning up babies costs more than it would cost to keep all the poets in America for a year.

Such questions are invidious and show a complete lack of understanding of people whose only response is, "Go away man, I just want to do nice things. I love everybody. Something is happening and you'll never know what it is."

What are the things the seceders accede to? Where and how are they *engagé*? In issues that directly effect the quality of life. The provos of Amsterdam are no different than the people in the East Village or San Francisco's Haight-Ashbury. They are against and will act in mass against the destruction of the environment by the automobile, the pollution of the atmosphere and waters, the censorship of art, drama, literature, they will act for all civil-rights and civil-liberties issues. They will even support trade-union action to organize the wage slaves in California agriculture—because this is a moral issue. Otherwise they are antagonistic to trade unions as part of a vicious system. They will fight for free theater and music in the parks. For neighborhood cultural centers—and of course in attacks by the Establishment on the Blacks—they appear in force.

The society is vulnerable to this kind of direct, personal spontaneous attack. If you put your hand in an old-fashioned gear box of a steam shovel, you will get it torn off. If you poke your finger into a million-dollar computer, it will shudder, choke, and break down. Four Negro boys walked into a cheap Southern restaurant and asked for hamburgers and sat and waited quietly—that was more than a decade ago. They began a process which nothing now can ever stop.

Similarly, poets and singers and even underground moviemakers are—each one—more subversive of the old society than any organization or party possibly could be anymore. And they have their own international. The London Scene is top-heavy with Americans—especially San Franciscans. Provos seem to go back and forth across the Channel every week. The Underground Press syndicate includes not only *The Berkeley Barb* and *The East Village Other,* but the London *International Times,* and *Peace News,* and papers in Amsterdam, Stockholm, Paris, and the Rhineland. Although they are many times as many, like the old Paris-London-America avant-garde around the Café Dôme in the Twenties, everybody seems to know everybody else—and wherever you go, you find friends who dig Gary Snyder, know where the best grass grows, and love all sentient creatures.

III.

Youth is The Man of the Year. Marihuana parties and Vietnam demonstrations are overwhelmed by sociology students with true-or-false questionnaires and by *Life* photographers. What passes for analysis of what is happening is usually based on vestigial remnants of the sectarian Marxism of the years between the wars, as appropriate to contemporary problems as the speculations of the Gnostics.

"What goes on? I really wanna know," says Donovan. First, the biological structure of the human race is changing. Most obviously man is growing younger. In both the wealthy and poor nations the majority of the population is under thirty, and soon the majority of the voting population will be in their twenties. Birth rates, death rates, infant mortality, age at sexual maturity, age at the onset of senescence, general health, causes of death, even height, weight, and condition of the teeth—all the statistics of public health have changed drastically in the last two decades and are still changing in the same directions. People under thirty don't look like members of the same nation as their grandparents.

Mental health statistics, records of commitments to mental hospitals, prison populations, out-patient cases of neurosis and psychosis, arrests for petty crimes and disorders, juvenile delinquency, seem to be moving in the opposite direction. Mostly this is due to better diagnosis and treatment and to more thorough policing of the society. It is simply not true that "the tensions of life are greater now than they were a century ago," as a reading of Engels' *Condition of the British Working Class* or any of hundreds of similar works on the slum poor and the workers in mines and mills of those days will prove.

The poor didn't have mental problems. Tension, like sexual intercourse in the old joke, was much too good for them. If they broke through the crust of society and disturbed their betters they were hauled off to court and jail. If they stayed in the slums they were allowed to stew in their own juice of crime undisturbed, or tried, convicted, and punished on the spot by the policeman's club.

Today a skilled mechanic in a Stockholm suburb lives better than Gustavus Adolphus; that we know, but we seldom realize that in many ways a Negro family in San Francisco on welfare payments in a subsidized housing project lives better than Charlemagne. Both can afford tensions and neuroses which only fifty years ago were the exclusive privilege of the Viennese mercantile aristocracy.

In the years since the Second World War our ways of life have changed drastically, but they have lagged just as drastically behind the changes in technology, as technology still lags behind the changes in science itself. The well-educated layman over forty seldom has any notion of what has happened in biology, physics, astronomy, cosmology, since he read the *ABC of Relativity* and the popular works of Eddington and Jeans, just as the suburban housewife who switches on her "electronic oven" has any idea of how it works, or still less, of what technology could really do to housekeeping if it got the chance. We are still destroying the environment with a machine, the internal combustion automobile engine, which is totally obsolete, from the steering mechanism to the sales organization to the political disgrace of the Arab peninsula. A billion people still have unwanted children year after year. We still inhale clouds of carcinogens to relax our nerves. We still drink alcohol in poisonous concentrations. We still murder "niggers" in America and "gooks" in Vietnam. One third of the population is still, as FDR said, ill clothed, ill housed, and ill fed—in the civilized countries. In the world, nine-tenths of the people still live lives that are nasty, brutish, and short, and grow steadily worse.

Here, in the foregoing paragraphs, lies the explanation of what's happening. The cybernetic, computerized, transistorized society is already here in potential and an ever-increasing number of people are insisting on walking into it and living there. We can afford peace, we can afford creative leisure, we can afford to demonstrate and revolt until we get them. A society in which hard labor is no longer the original source of value can afford to be good. The best and most effective demonstration is simply to start living by the new values. The people who do are going to outlive the people who don't unless the oldies murder them all in their wars.

The past year has witnessed a tremendous step up in the tempo and force of protest and a great clarification of objectives. First of course is the Vietnam War. It is no longer safe for spokesmen for the Credibility Gap, otherwise known as the U.S. State Department and Executive, to appear on college campuses. They are physically attacked and driven from the platform and have to be rescued by helicopter from cellar exits. One of the most popular buttons amongst young Americans reads, "Lee

Harvey Oswald, Where Are You Now That Your Country Needs You?" Students riot and go on general strikes when the Navy erects a recruiting booth on university property. You don't have to take my word for it—*Time* magazine says so too.

What would have happened had there been no Vietnam War? Much the same thing but at a slower tempo. Vietnam, like Voltaire's God, has been so convenient that, had it not have existed, it would have had to be invented. There is more than a stale joke here. All correspondents agree that the minute they land in Saigon, the brass overwhelms them with exhibitions of new hardware, like little children on Christmas morning. All wars, but Vietnam most especially, are characterized by a qualitatives change in the technology, a "great leap forward" in which "quantity changes into quality," to talk Marxist argot. Electronic search and destroy gimmicks above the jungles, and an indomitable demand to change completely the quality of life at home.

There are no Dutch troops in Vietnam, so the provos have been able to concentrate on resistance to the destruction of the environment by an outworn technology in the grip of mindless greed. From the point of view of an intelligent insect from Mars, there is a remarkable similarity. The fumes that make Amsterdam almost uninhabitable and the machines that clutter the streets and destroy all the advantages and pleasures of men living together in cities—these differ from napalm only in being slower in their effects—it is all gasoline in one form or another. For "politics" in Clausewitz' maxim, substitute "technology."

Against cigarettes, against hard alcohol, against sexual hypocrisy, against political fraud, against the commodity culture of conspicuous expenditure, against the dead hand of the past armed with a police truncheon that opposes all motion into the future—*for* the ancient theological virtues, voluntary poverty —the rejection of the destructive lures of a predatory society, the chastity of sexual honesty, and obedience to personal integrity . . . it is very convenient to the social critic that the youth of Amsterdam should have been able to define their program so clearly, unconfused by the vast evil that hangs in a cloud over America. Is this anarchism? If anarchism is the realization that the ballot is a paper substitute for the bullet, the bayonet, and the billy, that liberty is the mother, not the daughter of order, and that property in the means of life is robbery, it is anarchism. Certainly there is no important difference between the anti-programmatic programs of youth in Amsterdam, Stockholm, and San Francisco. The fundamentals stand out clearer in the smoggy air of Amsterdam, that is all. As jazz musicians say, we need a new book.

The great difference between Europe and America is on the other side, amongst the old whisky drinkers, as American youth now call them. Europe lies under a dictatorship of the aged. Willy Brandt, Günter Grass, Harold Wilson, these are professional young men grown old. Who represents "youth" in France? A mummified boy adventurer from the Chinese and Spanish Revolutions, a kind of political Jean Cocteau . . . really a horrifying vision. A politician like Kiesinger, who has been as carefully manufactured as a TV image as ever was Nixon, Kennedy, and Reagan, to whom is he manufactured to appeal to? The young? Indeed not. People all over recently were crying about the comeback of Nazism in the provincial elections. Kiesinger has been constructed to appeal to the stay put, not the come back. His publicity image is that of a kind of Tallyrand or Abbé Sieyes of a half-century of lost revolutions, wholesale betrayals, and genocide on all hands. His appeal is aimed at a target distinguishable by the same gleam of silver hair as his own head.

In America things are different. This is the land of highly developed consumer research. What's The Target? Youth. What's the hottest commodity along Mad Alley? Revolt. God knows, I was told that on Madison Avenue in the executive office of MCA ten years ago, when they wanted to take me over as a stellar attraction.

So the Republican rebirth in the November election was a kind of youth revolt . . . a revolt of aging youth who are entering income brackets they never knew existed until they got their tax forms. Illinois, Massachusetts, New York, Oregon, the winners were all presented as idealized junior executive types. Where this was impossible, as in the case of Reagan, who is about as old as I am, liberal applications of pancake make-up, Man-Tan, mascara, hair dye, pep pills, and the experience of a lifetime playing good cowboys produced a reasonable facsimile thereof, if not youth itself. Reagan's opponent, Pat Brown, looked old and tired and vulgar in his cradle.

Johnson the Second and his successors are old men with old ways and old solutions for old problems, whatever their ages. Most of them are men of the Cold War, if not of the New Deal, the Spanish Civil War, and the Moscow Trials. What everyone realizes, except themselves, about the Vietnam War is that, blood and horror disregarded, it is inappropriate—it is an obsolete answer. The 1968 national election was a contest (as will be the 1972) between the draft-card burners and the IBM branch managers, young youth against old youth . . . the audiences of Bob Dylan versus the audiences of Dave Brubeck. I think from the point of view of older societies, in both senses, American politics in the coming years is going to seem very odd indeed. The Declaration of Independence, the Communist Manifesto, *Mein Kampf,* these are totally obsolete as rhetorical manuals. The new styles are to be found in *Seventeen, Mademoiselle,* and *Playboy*. Or so the million-dollar public-relations firms believe. The backwash into Europe is going to be interesting to observe. Even more interesting is going to be the youth backlash—the response of the target itself. Besides being anti-anti-life, the young are also anti-manipulation, or is that the same thing?

1967–1969

11. Who Is Alienated From What?

For years alienation has been the favorite catch word of the American literary establishment, as triangulated by the *Partisan Review, Commentary,* and the *New York Review of Books.* What they mean is that since these establishment members lost their jobs in Army Intelligence after the war, the ruling circles of American society have forgotten they exist and no longer ask them out.

On the other hand, there has been growing up in Europe what amounts to a systematic philosophy or sociology of alienation. Several intellectual currents have converged to form what is today a stream of thought that is practically unchallenged. Since the publication of the philosophical notebooks of the young Marx just before the war, people who broke with the Communist Party but remained Marxists have come to emphasize the problem of alienation as fundamental.

From Kierkegaard to Sartre and Merleau-Ponty alienation has been a central concept of the Existentialists. In the tremendous intellectual upsurge in the Catholic Church that has followed Pope John's *aggiornamento,* modern Catholics have pointed out what has been obvious to everyone else for a long time, that anyone who tries to model his life on Christ and his apostles is by definition alienated from a predatory society.

Today the dialogue between these groups has begun to be overheard even within the ranks of the European Communist parties, most especially the Italian and Polish. The unorthodox Yugoslavs have been leaders in the movement for a long time. This discussion is where intellectual life is today in Europe, but it has had little influence in America. Even theoretical socialist magazines like *Dissent* or libertarian ones like *Liberation* devote little or no space to the discussion of alienation, and the middlebrow magazines are aggressively unaware of its existence.

Partly this is due to the American theory that general ideas are the exclusive province of college professors, hired to teach them for grades or theses. Partly it is the American, and particularly the American labor movement's lack of interest in anything but bread-and-butter issues, and partly it is due to the fact that in America today even an unfavorable serious discussion of ideas that have any connection with the name of Marx is immediately labelled Communist, and anyone who embarks upon such a discussion is in danger of investigation.

David Herreshoff in *American Disciples of Marx* comments on Earl Browder's farewell to Marxism, "Through Browder's *Marx and America* runs an implicit identification of the level of wages and the level of well-being of the workers. The Marxist concept of alienation is not once alluded to in this work purportedly concerned with the relevance of Marx to American experience." Browder's book is primarily an attack on the theory of progressive impoverishment. It never occurs to him that Marx gave a symbolic "material" existence to a moral critique of his society and that today his categories are deserting their materialist vestures and returning to their old etherealization.

Alas, the same is substantially true of Herreshoff's book itself, although Daniel De Leon, to whom Herreshoff gives most space, was acutely aware that human self-alienation was the very reason for being of the revolt against industrial civilization. Behind his unfortunate addiction to mixed metaphors in the William Jennings Bryan fashion, which apparently the age demanded, De Leon shows a better understanding of the fundamental problems raised by Marxism than Lenin, Kautsky, or Plekhanov. After the Third Congress of the Comintern, Left Communism's very memory has been effectually obliterated.

The present efforts of the American Left to reorganize itself are little influenced by the tremendous Marxist *aggiornamento* which has been sweeping the Iron Curtain countries, the French and Italian Left, and is even beginning to penetrate the sealed minds of the Workers' Fatherland itself. I used the word "*aggiornamento*" advisedly, because there has been a most remarkable convergence with the development of a new philosophy of man in the Roman Catholic Church. These two movements in fact are the most significant and exciting in contemporary Europe. In America there is a considerable number of Catholic thinkers who have launched a dialogue with the Marxist *aggiornamento.* As far as any answers have appeared they have come from across the Atlantic or from Japan. Certainly there has been little response from anybody identified with any Marxist party in America. This is curious indeed, because the entire movement of what has been called the "psychoanalytic Left" is American-based and is quoted constantly by Marxist writers trying to develop a contemporary philosophy of man in Yugoslavia, Poland, Japan, or Italy.

There are several reasons for this. American Marxism has been dominated for over a generation by a mindless, vulgar bureaucracy principally distinguished by a militantly execrable taste in all aspects of life and a scorn for thought of any sort. There is no essential difference in values and manners, between the bureaucrats of American Marxism, the House of Representatives, and any Board of Aldermen. They all represent the American Political Way of Life. It is the system of values known by this name which of course is what makes the alienated alienated.

An American theory of alienation significantly has come from practical clinicians, confronted every day in their practices with patients made profoundly sick by a scale of values which has for its summit the reduction of all things and all men to commodities. It is the treatment of the mentally ill with manifest moral lesions which has shifted the bases of psychoanalysis in America from the Sixth to the Tenth Commandment. The besetting sin of modern society is certainly not adultery—it is covetousness. In modern America it is so besetting that the average educated person encountering the word in the Bible believes it is some ritual violation peculiar to the ancient Hebrews, like eating crayfish.

The runaway pornography of the American entertainment business—including pseudo-highbrow publishers who concentrate on dope and homosexual prostitution—is not motivated by sex, but by the reduction of sex to a commodity whose advertising lures must be continuously escalated and which can never be satisfied. This is a commonplace. Since all critics of our society say this, it is strange that America has not developed what might be called a systematic philosophy of its own morbidity. Working psychiatrists, even of the psychoanalytic Left, still function in an atmosphere of pandemic pressure, like traumatic surgeons in an air raid. It's the laity who read the theoreticians—whether Erich Fromm, Leslie Farber, or Abraham Maslow.

An important factor in the failure of American socialism to produce any kind of philosophical Marxism is the profoundly uncongenial temper of Hegelianism to the dominant pragmatism and pluralism of American philosophy. There has not been a socially significant Hegelian thinker in America since Josiah Royce. It is interesting that behind his soft and well-bred prose lurk some extraordinarily revolutionary ideas, precisely those so influential in Europe today: his notion of the Absolute as the Beloved Community, and, of course, the doctrine of reification, the idea that the turning of men into things was the essence of alienation or original sin.

These ideas are central to the leaders of political *aggiornamento* in Yugoslavia or Italy, but in America any mass movement of head-on attack on alienation as such is largely confined to the most intelligent members of the notorious Revolt of Youth. The only trouble with the Revolt of Youth or the New Left is that it has been defenseless against its main enemy. It took only a year for that caricature of Big Business and the Big Business ethic—Organized Vice—to take over the Hippies; and the movement itself, by the pressure of idle youngsters of the upper middle class, was turned into a craze for the conspicuous expenditure of senseless commodities—beads, couch cover serapes, and worn-out squirrel skin chubbies. This is also the general tendency of American literature and art. Where Poland produces Gombrowicz staged by Growtowski, and France and Ireland cooperate in producing Beckett, we come up with Andy Warhol, just a messier variety of chic.

Who is alienated from what? The writings of the young Marx which discuss the subject and which have become so influential today are actually ambiguous and contradictory. At times Marx speaks as Hegel; alienation is the very principle of creativity, the Absolute self-alienates itself in creation. Sometimes he speaks of all work as alienating. Again he speaks of man engaged in what later he would call the commodity production of capitalism as being alienated from his product, from his fellows in work, and from the work itself. What he never mentions, but himself perfectly exemplifies, is the alienation of the intellectual, clerkly caste from the new ruling class. In this he was only the latest of a long line of *alienés* who began to appear contemporaneously with the rise of that class itself. This is an historically unparalleled phenomenon, characteristic only of Western European civilization since the rise of the middle class.

All important works of art, from the middle of the eighteenth century on, have rejected all the distinguishing values of the civilization which produced them. Rousseau, Blake, de Sade, Hölderlin, Baudelaire, Byron, Stendhal, these are only the most conspicuous and extreme *révoltés*. Not even the apostles of the middle class's own revolution—Marat, Robespierre, Saint Just—thought they were waging that revolution for the values of that class. If we project this situation back on the Rome of Virgil, the Greece of Sophocles, or the China of Tu Fu, its historical peculiarity is of course apparent. Catullus may be angry and neurotic but he is anything but alienated.

The clerkly caste had been as important in the Middle Ages as ever they had been in Egypt or Babylon. In a commercial, industrial civilization they became "minions," skilled servants deprived of self-determination, even more of a personal, determinative role in society. It is this sudden loss of power, and of personal autonomy, that has fed the wider concepts of alienation.

It is from literature and art that the alienated personality has spread, first to the technical and professional intelligentsia, the very pets of the society, and from them to an ever deepening stratum of the working class. The shocking exploitation—worse than chattel slavery—characteristic of British business enterprise in its primitive days, which was so well described by Engels and others—did not produce "alienation" in the intellectual sense of the word. The naked child dragging a coal cart in a narrow tunnel did not become alienated; he became dead. The young Marx—and seventy-five years after him, Trotsky, in *Literature and World Revolution*—often speak like William Morris. Creative intellectuals themselves, they imagined that if the work of the industrial worker could be made creative, like that of the artist, he would cease to be alienated.

As a matter of fact, my experience with industrial workers has led me to suspect that most of them do not resent the low level of personal participation in the production process. Charlie Chaplin may have considered a job on the assembly line destructive of the personality. This was not an opinion widely shared in the United Auto Workers Union, and now the assembly-line worker himself is disappearing. In a completely automated and computerized system of production, most of the small number of workers required would in fact be able to participate creatively. In the heaviest, and once most onerous, extractive industries this is already becoming true. But in the automated Western world, and equally in the socialized East, personal alienation increases, even amongst the most favored beneficiaries of the new society. Account executives and commissars mimic Baudelaire. As slavery was a substitute for machinery, Bolshevik "socialism" is a substitute for automation.

On the other hand, immense numbers of people are becoming physically alienated from productive society altogether. The word here should not be alienated, but redundant. As labor power steadily loses its role as the primary source of economic value, whole races and nations become redundant. Except for the Talented Tenth, the American Negro today is born alienated. His black skin has led him to being sifted down to the bottom of the economic pile where he has nothing to sell but his labor power, and that labor power, which once built railroads and picked cotton, finds no buyers. Africa and the rest of the former colonial world has been liberated because the metropoles, the former imperialist nations, have discovered that imperialism is unprofitable.

Where once the current of rejection of the dominant society flowed from the intellectuals down and out into the common people, today the current is reversed. Dick Gregory, James Baldwin, LeRoi Jones, Frantz Fanon, Charles Mingus, Miles Davis, the most militant artist spokesman for the alienated black common people, have themselves enjoyed specially favored upbringing and a plethora of endowments from the "power structure." They participate in modern society far more than most white intellectuals—with a vengeance. At least their vengeance strives to be creative. They are eminently successful and doing creative work. Society has discriminated in their favor. They are black. As black men the current of society's rejection and reciprocal rejection of society flows up from the unwanted black common people. The child coal picker in 1840 England may have died of overwork, but her work was needed. Nobody needs the thousands and thousands of unskilled workers who are now entering a third generation on welfare, housed, or rather economically embalmed and stowed out of sight, in housing projects and other slums. This is an entirely different kind of alienation from the one Marx diagnosed in the labor process. The conviction that "nobody wants me, nobody needs me, nobody knows I exist" may be the birthright of the ghetto, but it is coming to pervade all levels of modern society, even the most productive and favored.

At the top of the social heap the children of the upper middle class turn on, tune in, and drop out in herds and droves. This is true of the children of factory managers in East Berlin just as much as it is true of the girls from Sweetbriar wrapped in bedspreads and running barefoot in the Haight-Ashbury.

The most fashionable artists strive desperately to invent some new nihilism and sell it to idle rich women. Andy Warhol and

Kenneth Anger are far more fashionable with far richer people than ever was John Singer Sargent. The assumption is that when a rich woman spends $12,000 for a three-foot square of masonite painted an even coat of solid blue, or on a rusted, pressed automobile body, or on an exact ceramic reproduction of human feces, and puts the thing in her penthouse, it will destroy her. Unfortunately for the neo-Dadaist revolutionaries, she spends $12,000 or more a year on a psychoanalyst to keep that from happening, and never misses the money for either Dadaist or doctor.

Meanwhile, throughout the society, millions of mute inglorious people, surfeited with commodities and commodity relationships, become ever more divorced from their work, their fellows, their spouses and children, their lives and themselves.

"Why did you set all those fires?" "Why did you shoot thirty people on the university campus?" "Why did you kill those seven nurses?"

"I didn't know who I was." "I wanted to do something so that I could prove to myself I was really existing."

This goes all the way to the top. "Why are you dropping napalm on children?" "Why are you tempting a mighty nation to drop its hydrogen bombs on you?" Almost certainly the answer is, "I have the titles of power but I can't tell who I am."

1967

12. The Demagogic Process

I.

In his morning-after speech Dick Nixon's first pledge was to unify the country. This sounds nice but if he could bring it off peaceably it would certainly be the greatest trick of his career. We are actually faced with the same kind of irreconcilable division that existed at the elections of Lincoln and Wilson. They unified the country all right, or most of it, with the only measure that does unify a nation breaking down in hopeless antagonisms—war. It is war that is going to be a major threat for the next four years. Nixon as president certainly cannot be blamed for this. The Eisenhower administration left the country in about as peaceable a condition as could have been hoped, in spite of the atom rattling of Brinkman Dulles.

By and large the last Republican administration was the best proof of the practicality of anarchism in modern history. Ike gave the country something close to no government at all. Nothing went seriously wrong. True, we had a depression, mild enough by 1929 standards, but really just the deflationary program of the Eastern financial establishment. Ike exercised his executive only where it mattered. He always squashed Secretary Dulles as that gentleman drew near one of his many brinks. Certainly never in his administration was the country as close to war as it was twice over Jack Kennedy's Cuber.

Ike inherited a situation different from the present one. The second Truman administration was essentially a Labor Party administration characterized by the rabid Russophobia and Red-hunting of organized labor. Truman's policies were indistinguishable from those of the fatheaded old trade-union warhorse Ernie Bevin, Britain's Labor Foreign Minister, who was restrained from advocating a preventive war while Our Side had the atoms only by Nye Bevan's threat to throw the decision into the streets. However, when Ike took office the United States had an unchallengeable superiority over all the world. The country could afford peace. Where the Americans could not dictate they could at least "contain." Then too, compared with today, the domestic peace was profound, practically slumberous. Recession or no, America was reaping the first fruits of the new technology, the affluent society. After all, don't forget—the infamous McCarthy era was the Truman administration.

Everything today has changed. The American System of client states and interlocking alliances has broken down. SEATO has ceased to exist. In fact, certain former members might be called more active enemies of the United States within the limits of their weakness than are Russia and China in the security of their strength. Israel, America's bastion in the Middle East, is beleaguered, and, were Nasser crazy enough, could vanish in atomic smoke in a matter of minutes.

From Portugal to Taiwan the Americans hold power only by frightfully expensive subsidy of dictatorships, most of whom would be overthrown on the first morning of a general war. In addition, most of these juntas are made up of foolish criminal types who haven't got sense enough not to flaunt their thievery and even to sell "guns and butter" from America to their enemies. NATO has been outflanked by de Gaulle and consists in fact of West Germany and a large number of loquacious white-haired gentlemen in uniforms and morning coats at a large number of mahogany tables scattered here and there.

Yet in the past year as any West Point senior could tell you, Lyndon Johnson and Breshnev-Kosygin have moved their respective countries into attack positions. Heavy concentrations of Soviet troops within a short ramble of Munich and the immense American forces nearby are not postures of defense. Neither is the CIA stickup of Greece. The whole weight of the American strategy is shifting from Spain to Greece. Somebody woke up after almost thirty years to Churchill's advice about "the soft underbelly of Europe." As in so many wars before, the Balkan peoples are caught in this nutcracker. Don't think for a moment they don't know it. Even the most loyal Stalinists in the Balkans are running scared.

We had dinner recently with a Bulgarian Apparatchik, a typical representative of the Iron Curtain government most servile to Moscow. It took only a little wining and dining to reveal that he was scared and wished his country could be moved to some nice safe place like Saskatchewan. The only people whose lands are going to be fought over after the cities are gone who are thoroughly in favor of the belligerency of their masters are the East Germans. Even the West Germans at least talk "good neighbor policy." Still for the past two years the White House and the Kremlin have advanced their pawns into ever more threatening positions. So far the gambits have been declined by both sides.

This is the chessboard that Dick Nixon takes over. Both sides have played a variety of risky threatening openings and now the pieces are all deadlocked. This is a situation in chess where even the most conservative players are tempted to do something rash. The President of the United States for the next four years is going to have to be a man of intelligence, patience, skill, and cool nerve. Breshnev-Kosygin is, I mean are, bad actors, maybe, but they are not Helen Gahagan Douglas and they can't be tricked. There'd *better* be a "new Nixon." He can't end his career as he began it or we'll all end with him.

The French fascists liked to scrawl on the walls "OCCIDENT!" They're right. It's still The West that's going to make the difference. The Vietnam War may have destroyed the morale of America and corroded the American conscience perhaps past repair just as the Boer War did the English. It is a horrible and shameful thing and the worst thing about it is that it is unnecessary and foolish. If the powers behind Nixon are now, as I think they are, the Eastern financial establishment and the old basic industrial wealth, it should be fairly easy to get out of Southeast Asia. We'll see when we know the personality of the Cabinet. Cooling the new Watch on the Rhine and the Danube is going to take some doing. Of course, there is one thing even a lame duck can do and that's push the red button and go out in a blaze of glory. Whatever his many faults, Nixon is not a loquacious fool, so we could have done worse.

II.

I have said elsewhere that all over the world nations with assorted antagonisms, but most especially Russia and the United States, were moving into attack position; that Russia and the United States were already heavily invested in a condominium of the planet—and incidentally the solar system—and that this was shown by the total collapse of all the Moscow-line Communist Parties all over the world as even mildly radical much less "anti-imperialist" organizations. In America, people who believed J. Edgar Hoover are still running around talking about the Menace of Moscow, but this is just due to the invincible ignorance of provincialism. Amid all the uproar on the campuses, much of it revolving around demands by Black students, where is the late lamented DuBois Club once the *bête noir* in every sense of the academic establishment?

These two political tendencies, the dominant ones in the world today, are reciprocal. It's not a condominium unless both partners are equally invested and have equal power. There is shutting down over the world a dictatorship of the nineteenth century. It is a commonplace of economic theory that Russia is very far from being "a soviet union." It is a system of state capitalism designed to force a reluctant population through the period of economic development described as capitalism by

Karl Marx. Today in England, France, and the United States the state is assuming an ever-increasing control of the economy, not for the purpose of moving society on into the age of transistors, cybernetics, and a relevant financial system but for driving society back into the mechanical-industrial-banking system that broke down in August 1914. Those countries which have resisted this forced archaization are the healthiest socially, economically, and, with one exception, culturally in the world: Sweden, Switzerland, and, to a much less degree, Benelux and, suddenly awakening and coming up behind, Canada—but most of all East and West Germany. In 1946 Germany was in ruins and about half of the technical and professional cadres who should have been running the country in twenty years were dead. The Americans pumped millions into West Germany while the Russians did everything possible to keep the East crippled and humiliated. Today the second most economically powerful nation in the West is West Germany. The second most powerful economically in the East is East Germany. The reason is very simple. Of the old time Great Powers the two Germanies are the only nations who have tried even approximately to realize the technological potential and the administrative and financial concomitance of the second half of the twentieth century. At least for socially wholesome goals. The cybernetic revolution in Russia and the United States is used mostly for tricks like photographing the moon's backside or for computerizing the dossiers of dissidents. De Gaulle wants to go back to *Louis d'Or*. Dicky's tricky attorney general and his assistants have managed to advocate, of course in the Aesopian language of ultra-democratic demogogy, the suspension or abolition of each paragraph of the Bill of Rights.

What about Ulbricht? The disgusting vulgarity of the Ulbricht dictatorship is so easy to explain. The economic revolution in East Germany, by which I don't mean anything one hundred years old like Marxism, has proceeded so far that there is nothing left for the Russians' quislings to do but kick around artists and writers. Here lies the secret of what's happening everywhere. As even Hugh Hefner knows and tirelessly says, the technological universe which is open before late twentieth-century man has made apparent to all who can really think and feel the promises of the new and greater meaning to life. The anal-retentive, work-and-slave, pray-and-save, you'll-get-pie-in-the-sky-by-and-by society of the mechanical industrial age has become morally intolerable besides, of course, becoming self-evidently lethal. It has become apparent to those who think and feel. Who thinks? Who feels? Damn few people who have survived and made it in the industrial, mechanical world with its business ethics. But the unthinking and the unfeeling are terrified of those who think and feel and who know that the present world is deadly and morally rotten. So they, not the young, have passed over to the attack. There are no pictures of fat cops lying on the ground on campuses and being kicked in the face by coeds.

A wire-editor friend of mine once told me that he estimated that on any given day there were approximately 700 student riots around the world. They riot at Brandeis, they riot at Kabul. Have the Afghan students been corrupted by John Dewey and Herbert Marcuse? The initiative is *not* coming from youth. The initiative is the moral attack on youth of an outworn century. Mr. Kissinger's heroes are Metternich, who held Europe under a reign of White Terror for a generation after the defeat of the French Revolution, and Bismarck who embarked Germany on the course of national suicide that led to the Nibelungen death of the Third Reich in flame and horror, whether in Hamburg and Dresden or in Auschwitz and Dachau. They have a plan, the plan of the Holy Alliance that put back together again with paper pins the Europe of the *ancien régime.* The trouble with youth, even the neo-Marxists of the SDS or the Negritude nationalists of the BSU, is they have no plan, they have only the future; but the future may never be.

The old technology could operate in a society whose golden rule was the sum total of individual evils will produce the greatest social good. This is the philosophy of Adam Smith and Ricardo, the business economists, but it is also the philosophy of Marx and Lenin, a *laissez-faire,* dog-eat-dog and devil-take-the-hindmost technology which operated by the mass accumulation of accidents with no idea of where it was going. Marx's or Lenin's greatest term of contempt was "Utopian Socialism." A cybernetic economy must so plan that every time you punch the computer you must have a clear idea of what you want out of the future. The transistor demands Utopia. For the next four years all progressive forces in America are going to be subject to relentless attack which they will not be able to meet by throwing rocks at cops. Most of the leaders will probably be in jail serving long sentences within a year. What has happened to the Black Panthers will happen next to the BSU and next to SDS and next Mark Rudd and the Yippie leaders and next to Allen Ginsberg and then Herbert Marcuse and Paul Goodman and then I would be quite insulted if not me as the twentieth century is forced to go underground or is confined behind barbed wire. We can spend our time as the nineteenth-century Russians who were sent to Siberia for struggling against the dark ages spent theirs in deciding what kind of society we want. Cybernetics won't work unless you begin by extrapolating. Revolution for the hell of it ends in the gas chamber or the gas oven. Everybody's running around yelling but it's all purely defensive. The offensive consists in having objectives so clear they are overpowering. Utopia belongs to us. We can't leave it to Timothy Leary or even estimable and diligent Hugh Hefner.

III.

Perhaps the apologists for violence in the Roman arena, television, the funny papers, the movies, and limited wars have something. Perhaps if the human race cannot discharge its hostilities periodically hostility festers within the body politic and eventually poisons all its organs and tissues. I don't think there is much doubt but that we would have had a major war long since if it had not been "impossible." Eventually of course we will have it with its "unthinkable" consequences but so far it has been averted by sheer fear with all the resulting frustrations that come from the lack of quick, easy, lethal solutions. Frustration and hostility have spread throughout the human race and have become the accepted way of life. Organizations and movements that started out internationalist, socialist, nonviolent, pacifist, are today violent, competitive, and nationalist externally, and internally they are ridden by unprincipled power struggles and interpersonal hostility. The guardians of law and order have lost all objectivity and are ruled by personal hatred. International politics more and more becomes not an ordinary old-fashioned power struggle but a deadly chess game of vindictive reprisals. CORE was an offshoot of the FOR, The Fellowship of Reconciliation, a religious pacifist organization, and its principal founder, Bayard Rustin, is ceaselessly attacked as an Uncle Tom—but what would happen if the founders of the Communist International or the Zionist movement came back to life in a meeting of their descendants?

Beside the chronic hostility of international, intergroup, and interpersonal relations there has developed out of the destructive waste of natural resources in the Second War (when, typically, virgin forests in California were cut down to make logs for corduroy roads in the New Guinea jungle which were then passed over by air transport and finally the airplanes were burned up rather than flown home) a new kind of exploitation of the environment. Just as all arts were supposed to approach the condition of music, so now all business enterprise tends to approach extractive industry. Pinchot's slogan, "The forests are a crop, not a mine" has been reversed. Businesses are treated as mines, not crops. "Get it and get out" and "It will last my time," once the business ideology of Latin America and the colonial world, has now instinctively been adopted by the business community of the metropoles. Where once only Guatemalan buccaneers and Persian generals had Swiss accounts, now in America they are changing from a status symbol like a Mercedes 700 to a commonplace like a Diners Club card. Travelling about the world today the most conspicuous single thing is the universal destruction of the environment. Lake Erie is an open sewer. Deep in the Alps the Italian lakes are polluted. Over a mile in the air Lake Arrowhead lies under a thousand feet of smog. The earth is being exploited with no regard for future generations. Is this because nobody believes there are going to be future generations?

Within any of the contexts now operating none of the major problems of the world is solvable. It's not just that the overpopulation of Latin America is at the mercy of the Pope and that the director of birth control in India does not believe in birth control; we forget that the Kennedy administration, one of the few relatively honest ones in American history, had broken down in complete frustration and pessimism months before the President was assassinated and similarly Khrushchev, who seems really to have tried to straighten things out in Russia, failed. The Johnson administration thrashed around like a longhorn steer caught in a mudhole and only made matters worse.

There is no sign anywhere that anyone in power wants to do something about this state of affairs. The commentators of the kept press tell us that the Nixon cabinet is made up of enlightened middle-of-the-road businessmen and they should be given a chance. They are nothing of the sort. Each one of them is on record as a representative of the politics of defiance, from the Secretary of the Interior who is fully as anti-conservationist as Eisenhower's man who seriously suggested leasing the national parks to private enterprise, to the Secretaries of State and War (Defense) who are advocates of "all necessary measures." Like Ronald Reagan and his minion Hayakawa the Nixon administration has already lined itself up into positions for a politics of showdown, of final confrontation. But it's the same everywhere. Straus is moving into position to take over the German chancellorship. Representatives of the *force du frappe* of the House of Rothschild already dominate the French cabinet. And did you ever notice as he has grown older that Richard Nixon no longer looks like the rather handsome Rudolph Hess. What he looks like now is a print taken from the combined negatives of Breshnev and Kosygin. What is going to happen in a world where every nation, every pressure group, and millions and millions of individuals move consciously and inexorably towards deadlock?

All hell is going to break loose.

It's apparently what people want. Certainly the Left, the students, the Negroes, all welcome confrontation. More and more people subscribe to the doctrine of "the worse, the better." "Once Dirty Dick starts his fascist repression then the movement will really mean business." On the other side Hayakawa tam o'shanters sprout like Mercedeses in San Marino, Montecito, Hillsborough, and Piedmont. The only trouble with all this is its mindlessness. None of the battalions on either side has any kind of program. Honky is always saying to the Black militants, "What is it you want?" and getting nothing but obscene abuse in return. Mark Rudd, the leader of the students at Columbia, has said in so many words, again and again, that their program is completely summed up in the words, "Up Against the Wall, Motherfucker!" This is not sarcasm, it's true. Herbert Read, Paul Goodman, A. S. Neill are dismissed as ideologues of the Old Left and there is not the slightest vestige of demands for a truly enlightened and progressive education. The amazing thing is that the student Left actually accepts monstrosities like the University of California, Columbia, or San Francisco State. They just want chittlins and maws in the cafeteria or classes in Swahili, the artificial *lingua franca* of the slave trade. The whites don't even want anything. But the same thing is true on an international scale. Go to some big library and get out the old publications of the Communist International and compare them with the stuff emanating from or inspired by Moscow or Peking today. The total lack of principle and Marxist theory in the contemporary literature is astonishing. As for American principles, they will be provided by a large staff of whiz kids on loan from a business that has made billions telling the public that black is white, cigarettes don't cause cancer, and whisky is good for young girls. Of course if you want principles you can always go to Czechoslovakia but you better get one of those rings with a couple of grains of cyanide of potassium in it. (1968!) You're going to need it. Casey Jones has become every man's ideal.

IV.

It was surprising to me at least how many people got all wrought up about the election when it finally came around. We didn't stay up to listen to the radio or watch television. I can't imagine an intelligent person being in the least concerned which utterly amoral vulgar demagogue got into the White House. It is some consolation that a silly and loquacious man who betrayed every principle he ever had was kept out. I hope his refusal so much as to come to the telephone when his opponent phoned him from the fifteenth floor that his staff were being mayhemed by the criminal pigs of the Hog Butcher of the World haunts him to his dying day. I hope he hears his own flatulent voice calling Pedernales from where the attack had been ordered, "Shall I or shall I not interfere, Massa?" every night as he falls asleep. One thing you can say for Dick Nixon, he's never had any principles to betray. He was the first of the robot politicians manufactured from used Rice Crispies coupons in the PR offices. We can look forward to four years of struggle between J. Walter Thompson, Chase, and Citibank and the hoodlum millionaires of Southern California over the control of the country. It would be interesting if they would all insist on a purely robot government with Reagan, Murphy, Shirley Temple in the cabinet, Rin Tin Tin in HEW, and King Kong as Secretary of Defense. It remains to be seen. One of the peculiarities of the modern demagogic process with its McLuhan destruction of reality is that last time it permitted the election of perhaps the only man in the history of the American presidency who could be called positively evil. We have had fools and rascals, Van Burens, Chester A. Arthurs, and Hardings, but Johnson was unique. There is something about the electoral process and the public mind that until his day kept a man like him out of the presidency. Is Nixon evil? Metaphysicians have said that evil is privative, that it is the intrusion of not-being into being. I suppose in this case Nixon is evil because like all the not-people he doesn't exist. However, the first "government by manufactured celebrity" was that of Jack Kennedy. He was just manufactured by a nicer advertising agency. Perhaps the day will soon come, what with all this talk of reforming the method of presidential elections and getting rid of the Electoral College, that the American people won't have to vote for the package, they'll just vote for an advertising agency as now they vote for electors.

The most important news of the election in San Francisco was the extremely low vote for Kathleen Cleaver, lower than that polled by Anita Whitney or Oleta O'Conner ever on the old-time Communist ticket in the Red Thirties. The fact that her vote almost exactly matched Paul Jacobs would indicate that she got no votes from the indomitable suffragettes who always vote for a woman regardless and that she got no race votes as such. Oleta could always rely on a big hunk of both the women and the Irish. Not only that, but Kathleen Cleaver is certainly the best-looking woman ever to run for public office in San Francisco and at least as highly cultured as the notoriously cultured Missus Onassis. She got six votes in the four polls in my Black neighborhood.

What went wrong? It is very simple. The Panthers and the Peace and Freedom Party simply made no connection at all with what they used to call the masses, least of all the Black masses. Their appeal was confined almost exclusively to displaced persons—unemployed Black youth, hippies, and rich bohemians in Pacific Heights. I saw it coming. All the past year the high-school boys in the Black neighborhood where I live were going about in black berets and black-leather jackets. Then the Panthers opened a headquarters around the corner. Within a week they had scared off all these young fellows who would have been invaluable to them. This was not just due to their wild talk about shooting every honky on the Day of Motherfucker. It was due to their closed-tight cliqueishness, like a gang invading somebody else's turf. For a half mile in every direction the neighborhood is from 75 to 95 per cent Black, but it is a neighborhood of Black working men and working wives and their reaction to the Panthers shocked even me with the violence of its wrath.

I'm not blaming anybody. I'm just saying this isn't the way to run a revolution or even start one. Who believes Willie Brown is a Tom? Certainly not the working people in his Assembly district. Most people who know him consider him the most enlightened, well-educated, and dedicated politician in the city. He is almost as cultured as Kathleen herself. By choosing to run her, the product of one of the most fashionable schools in the country, and of course a person who would be considered white in any other country on earth, as a representative of the Black dispossessed against "Uncle Tom Willie," the Peace and Freedom Party and the Panthers simply defied themselves into isolation. It is so easy to believe that the people who turn out for a demonstration and make a lot of noise are going to vote—or even stay around if push comes to shove in the most literal sense in the demonstration. Most of the following of the Peace and Freedom Party simply doesn't play any kind of determinative role in the society. They are redundant. Students and young Blacks are the unneeded people in the technological society and they are dumped into universities and government projects just like the older industrial capitalism dumped unwanted commodities into the colonies and finally into the sea or burned them up in war as now they burn up youth, Black and white. The French May Days proved, as contrasted to their German sympathetic reflection, that you can't exert power if you can't form alliances with people the society can't get along without. Until the longshoreman, the teamster, and the housepainter and their wives, two practical nurses, and a factory worker who live in the flat next to me can be convinced that the largely estimable program of the Panthers and the Peace and Freedom Party has some connection with them and that the persecution of Eldridge Cleaver or Huey Newton or Bobby Seale is a persecution of them, nothing is going to happen. There just aren't enough people outside the system. Black unemployment in California may be twice that of white but for the last couple of years that has been only 6 per cent, and 3 per cent is the necessary functional labor turnover of full production totalling all categories. In unskilled employment it is considerably higher. In other words, 94 per cent of the Black working-class population of California is working at any given time. They may want Black power, but only in that context can they be convinced of it. If they think Black power will destroy the context itself, they aren't going to buy it. Black power, Black culture, Black art, Black theater, Black poetry are all fine but what's important is not what blonde college girls think about it but what ordinary Black people do. Whether Eldridge Cleaver or LeRoi Jones, the question is, "What has Ray Charles or Muddy Waters got that I haven't?" Who's afraid of Muddy Waters?

1967–1968–1969

13. Back to the Sources of Literature

Many people—philosophers, philosophers of history, sociologists, anthropologists—believe that our civilization is undergoing a great turn like the change that took place in human life with the invention of agriculture or the development of city living or the use of metals. At such times the meanings of life change and human relationships undergo far-reaching reorganization. Almost all students of the sciences of man agree that we are passing from an industrial, mechanical age to a technological one in which many of the values, the guiding principles, of our society are being totally changed from plus to minus and vice versa. Wholesale overturns like this show themselves in the arts and in religion, immediately after the changes in technology, usually well before changes in political structure, and in the social codes to which men cling long after they have become irrelevant. This is obvious in the plastic arts. All you have to do is look to see that contemporary artists in every medium are after something quite different, not just from Raphael and Rembrandt, but from Picasso, or the Surrealists. This is not so apparent in literature. The printed page and the Academy shelter centuries-old vested interests. Things go on as usual with the inertia of the ages. Most people do not even notice what is happening in the art of poetry for the simple reason that it never occurs to them that what is happening is poetry.

City living, written literature, abstinence, saving, hard work all grew up together. Today, the most significant poetry, though not perhaps the best by older standards, is no longer created for the printed page. As in the days before the city and the alphabet, poetry has become once again an art of direct communication, one person speaking or singing directly to others. Along with this change has come, in the words of the poems themselves, a constant, relentless, thoroughgoing criticism of all the values of industrial, commercial civilization. Poetry today is people poetry as it was in tribal society and it performs the same function in a worldwide counter-culture. It is the most important single factor in the unity of that counter-culture and takes the place of ideologies and constitutions, even of religious principles. As such those whose lives are identified past recall with the older dominant culture certainly are justified in seeing it as profoundly subversive. Where is this poetry? It is in the lyrics of rock singers, protest singers, folk singers, and the singers of gathering places like the French *cafés chantants* now spread all over the world.

The interesting thing about this kind of poetry is that although it is the voice of a new culture that promises soon to overtake and surpass the old, it is itself not new. Its roots go back in our civilization to the Middle Ages. The difference today is that it is no longer the voice of an outcast minority but of "everybody under thirty" from Tokyo to Rome, from Baghdad to Trinidad to Nome.

Carl Orff's what shall we call it—parade-oratorio—*Carmina Burana* has made the largest collection of medieval student songs, songs of protest, erotic love songs, and hymns of bohemian life known to an immense number of people throughout the world. As a musical composition it may be glossy, what an older generation called a semi-classical number, but the music does swing and the lyrics in translation usually come with the record. They are poems of youth, of people who had opted out of the rigid, authoritarian medieval society, and they were sung in wine cellars and beer stubes by wandering students while they gambled at backgammon and gamboled with their doxies. In recent years the musical shorthand called neumes, written between the lines in the ancient manuscripts, has been deciphered and the reconstructed music can be heard on records. One thing about the music for sure, it rocks with the rhythms of dance. The lyrics say the same thing that poet singers in the student hangouts in the Paris Latin Quarter say today.

The tradition is uninterrupted, still there in the same place since the day there first were students in Paris. Later in the Middle Ages, in French, Villon is the very archetype, the poet laureate of 500 years of the counter-culture. So clearly does he speak for a way of life that his name has become a common noun and adjective in European languages.

At the very beginning of the Middle Ages in Provence there grew up a vast literature of both written and sung poetry that reflected the life of a society more permissive than any to be seen in Europe until modern times. The songs of the troubadours have connections with the poetry of sexual mysticism which spread from India to Persia and across Islam to Muslim Spain. Their influence spread then to Germany, England, even to Constantinople. Whether it was part of the Albigensian heresy or not, the entire culture of Provence, the most civilized part of Europe, was obliterated in the Albigensian Crusade, the bloodiest war of extermination in the West until the invention of gunpowder. Today the influence of the troubadours on a few modern poet singers is apparent, but in the intervening centuries the connection was snapped. The same sexual mysticism can be found in the songs of Leonard Cohen or Anne Sylvestre, both of them strongly influenced by troubadour songs.

It is not surprising that the high bohemianism of the courts of France, Burgundy, and Italy should have developed forms of expression that owed so much to the poor bohemianism of the wandering students. The court of France's most Renaissance king, François the First, was not unlike our modern jet set or the titled hippies of Way Out London. Bohemianism has been defined as the behavior of those who imitate the luxuries of the rich while lacking the necessities of the poor. If so, the high bohemianism of the rich simply imitates the counter-culture of the dropped-out poor.

A hundred years before Villon, songs of this type had already begun to penetrate to courtly circles as is shown by the first recorded comic operetta—*Le Jeu de Robin et Marion* by Adam De la Halle.

Love songs of the Renaissance are still sung in the *cafés chantants* today, and I remember when I was a little boy Yvette Guilbert, the great *diseuse* so often portrayed by Toulouse-Lautrec, singing Ronsard's "When you are old and seated by the fire" while the café full of diners and drinkers wept. Of course all lyric poetry voices such sentiments—"eat, drink, and be merry for tomorrow we die"; "hurry up and jump into bed, we're not going to last forever"; "getting and spending we lay waste our powers." The great secret, the difference between the straight world and the counter-culture, is that the latter takes seriously the ethics of lyric poetry, in fact can be said to make a world view of it. Whether that lyric poetry is sung by Japanese geishas, Chinese sing-song girls, black hustlers in New Orleans in 1910, or the displaced youth of 1941–1950 Paris who, if they had money, hung out in the cellars of the Latin Quarter and the Faubourg St. Germain and if they didn't, slept under bridges, hustled up a bottle of cheap wine, huddled around a salamander (an oil-can stove), and sang till they were tired enough to make love and fall asleep under newspapers. It was from those who were literally outcasts from society, displaced persons, whether homeless European youth or hustlers in the black ghettoes of the United States, that the significant poem-songs, the whole idiom of direct communication, people poetry, has grown. Both black America and the French cities have always possessed a thoroughly bohemianized working class, something no other cultures have had to the same degree. By the thirties of the last century, when the French Restoration had dispossessed huge numbers of the old clerkly castes and thrown them into the arms of the poor, a style of life and its expression in song were well developed. The same thing happened in New Orleans when the educated Creoles of color were dispossessed and thrown into the black ghettoes. "My folks was all Frenchmens" said Jelly Roll Morton playing piano in a brothel.

Charles Cros, the inventor of the phonograph, was the most popular poet-singer of this kind in mid-nineteenth-century Paris, and his poems spoke for a way of life completely unassimilable by the money-crazy, hypocritical, debauched, and puritanical society of Louis Napoleon's gimcrack Second Empire.

It is out of people like Charles Cros, simple, sensuous, lyrical, and sarcastic, that poets like Verlaine come, and all of those that he, Verlaine, first called "*poètes maudits,*" the cursed, the outcast poets, Germain Nouveau, Arthur Rimbaud, Alfred Jarry, Tristan Corbière, Jean Richepin. All of these poets are still sung. All you have to do is to look at their verse on the page to see that structurally it owes everything to the café song. Meanwhile there were other poets who wrote directly for such outlets, like the bitter poet of the outcast poor, the *clochards* and beggars who sun themselves along the Seine on the Quai de Montebello in the summer and sleep over air vents, covered with newspapers to shed the snow in winter—Jehan Rictus. Even more popular and still popular today was Aristide Bruant, the man in the black cape and slouch hat with the long red scarf down his back in the famous poster by Toulouse-Lautrec. The poster was an advertisement for Bruant's own café on Montmartre, the Mirliton, a major center of bohemian Paris in the Eighties and Nineties. Perhaps still the greatest record of the brief period after the war when St. Germain was in flower is *Germaine Montero chante les chansons d'Aristide Bruant* and on it is his greatest poem, *Rodeuse de Berges,* the perfect distillation of the heartbreak and loneliness of a little French tart without a man. It is very significant that this poem in everything but the three-line form is precisely a city blues of the type that was moving from New Orleans up the Mississippi city by city to Chicago in the same years. The liner notes on this record are by Pierre MacOrlan of the Académie Goncourt. Well they might be, for MacOrlan's poetry is of the same scene a generation later. Most of MacOrlan's poems are semi-narrative; e. e. cummings' sonnets about prostitutes imitate them directly. It too along with that of Francis Carco and others who spoke for the poor, the bohemians, and the underworld of Paris is still popular, still sung, where most of the literary poets, their contemporaries in the first third of the twentieth century, are already forgotten.

After the war Raymond Queneau and Jacques Prévert, who greatly resemble our own Lawrence Ferlinghetti, became immensely popular. Their books outsold most novels. In 1948 everybody under thirty-five seemed to have read Prévert's *Paroles* and you could see almost as many people with it on the subway as with the newspaper. It was impossible to spend an evening in any club on Rue St. Germain without hearing two or three of his pieces sung.

It should be borne in mind that all of this work, from Charles Cros on, was done by professionals. Alongside it, underneath it, floating as on a sea, were city folk songs produced by the actual poor, the outcasts, and the underworld themselves. The repertory of a girl who hung around the all-night and early-morning spots by Les Halles—the ones where the tourists did not go to eat snails and drink onion soup—was fabulous, comparable to that of any New Orleans or Chicago blues singer. Not only would she know hundreds of hustlers' songs, many by herself, many comic, most obscene, and all of them sad, but she also would know the most popular numbers by Prévert or Bruant—or Verlaine.

It is out of Occupied and Post-War Paris, the world of hunger, concentration camps, and displaced persons, most of the latter young and utterly penniless, that the golden age of St. Germain des Prés began. Once it got under way it came like an explosion. The great poets of Post-War II France are without exception the singers. Poets like Leo Ferré, George Brassens, Jacques Brel, Anne Sylvestre are incomparably better than the leading literary poet of the establishment, the flaccid Yves Bonnefoy who, after a thousand five-hundred years of French culture, manages to write as though he had just been graduated from a course in creative writing in an American university. Brassens is probably the first person who established the popular singer as a pivotal point of the counter-culture. When Bob Dylan was still a very little boy all the hip youth of France imitated the narrow beard Brassens then worn along his jaw line and they sang his songs while dashing about, a bird on her perch, on their one-cylinder bikes. The great secret of Brassens is that he speaks for the hard-core unassimilables with complete self-awareness. He knew that he and behind him his ever-growing following could not, and never would be, assimilated, and he knew why, and he said so in every song, whatever that song was about. With him the counter-culture comes of age and makes a bid, not for power, but for position. "We already understand history, the problem is to change it, not by politics but by a revolution of the human sensibility."

Any radical political leadership becomes part of the establishment—as was all too obvious in the May Days in Paris, both in 1958 and 1968. The real leadership passes not to "leaders" but to *spokesmen.* It is significant that the Marxist parties of France are absolutely opposed to conscientious objection, yet one of the most popular Philips records is *Le Deserteur,* sung by Boris Vian and thirteen *Autres Chansons Pacifistes.* Most of the people on the record are members of the older generation, the people over thirty-five who are never to be believed. These are the heroic age of St. Germain des Prés—Mouloudji, Les Frères Jacques, Juliette Greco, Jacques Brel, and Leo Ferré amongst others. Not only are these people responsible for the greatest renaissance of song in modern times, but they are responsible for the great cultural change of the counter-culture, the replacing of the acquisitive appetite with the lyric sensibility. Today their descendants in France are legion.

Even singers of popular love songs like Eva and Françoise Hardy sing about a kind of love, a kind of interpersonal relationship which implies a total restructuring of society. These girls are directly related to American singers like Judy Collins and Joni Mitchell, both of them disciples of Leonard Cohen, but before we can talk about them we have to go way back and trace the evolution of their kind of thing to its American roots.

Where do the lyrics of rock, folk rock, protest, and contemporary folk song come from? They come, as is obvious from their name, from black rock and roll, once called "rhythm and blues" and before that called "race records"—not the jazz singers of white night clubs, but of black pool halls, bars, athletic club dances, cheap dancehalls, crossroad sand shuffles. The white folk music style goes back to Scotch and

English folk song, the so-called Child Ballads (first exhaustively collected by Francis James Child in five large volumes at the end of the last century) and the first musical field research, the music mostly from Cecil Sharpe's two collections (*English Folk Songs,* mostly the ballads in Child, and *English Folk Song in the Southern Appalachians*). These are the versions still used by the most popular folk singers today along with others collected by John Jacob Niles and by the Library of Congress program under the direction of Allan Lomax. Today the literature of American folk songs, both native and of British origin, is illimitable, beyond measure. Alongside this traditionally accepted type of folk song there is the urban folk song which divides into several groups, mostly occupational—college boys, newspapermen, Greenwich Village bohemians, structural-steel workers. Many of these are very bawdy indeed, and for a long time were available only in emasculated versions in Carl Sandburg's *Song Bag* or in Frank Shay's *My Pious Friends and Drunken Companions.* Then there are work songs almost entirely confined to the more footloose occupations—sailors, cowboys, miners, lumberjacks, canal bargemen, hammermen, railroaders. These shade into the first songs of protest, largely the work of I.W.W. singers like Joe Hill, who were poets and organizers at once. Most Socialist, or later Communist, songs were political in emphasis, and most of them were imported from abroad. The songs of the Wobblies are still sung because they were not. The I.W.W. was an anarchist-syndicalist industrial union largely confined to those who were outside the dominant society altogether—migratory workers in the Plains States and Far West struggling against the barbarous conditions of mining, lumbering, and agriculture on what was still a frontier, and foreign-born textile and steel workers in the East, few of whom voted. Perhaps it is of the essence of a commercial and industrial society that it is not folkloristic and that folk songs come only from classes of the population which are alienated by nature, outside the society by choice and antagonistic to it, or who are involuntary outcasts, and so forced into more "natural" relationships just to survive.

There are all sorts of legends of how things get started in show business. For instance, all the big bands from Tin Pan Alley were supposed to have tooled up for a craze for Japanese music early in the Thirties (like the Hawaiian one of years before) but then the Japanese army fired on the U.S. destroyer *Panay* and a wave of anti-Japanese hysteria swept the country. Everybody's book had to be junked and there was nothing to take its place except last year's numbers. The jazz bands were the only ones that were rehearsed and ready to go—hence the Swing Era which came at a time when everyone assumed that big band jazz was dead forever. I don't know if this is true but it is certainly true that the popularity of American folk music with the general public begins with the singing of *The Prisoners' Song* in concert and on the vaudeville stage. The Victor record of Vernon Dalhart singing *The Prisoner's Song* with *The Wreck of the Ninety-Seven* on the flip was a runaway bestseller in the very early Twenties. Just at the moment that Tin Pan Alley commercialism was stifling the Heroic Age of the American Ballad, this moment coincided with the swift spread of radio sets into even the poorest homes. Soon there was hillbilly music everywhere. In the beginning a good deal of this was traditional folk song, but since part of the traditional repertory of the Southern mountain folk singers was the topical song for which obviously the words would have to be written by somebody, songs like *Floyd Collins, The Wreck of the Shenandoah, Lucky Lindy, O'er the Sea O'er the Sea Like an Eagle,* and ballads of contemporary desperadoes, murders, and hangings (one on Bonnie and Clyde was a masterpiece and it's a pity it didn't get into the movie), immediately became popular on the local stations in the Southern hill country and soon pushed the ancient songs and ballads that had come from England and Ireland into the background. Also certain very popular singers had the unscrupulous habit of copyrighting both music and text of songs which had come down from as early as the fifteenth century.* The locally produced topical ballad and love song was soon taken up by Tin Pan Alley and produced by indigent intellectuals from Greenwich Village who had never seen and never would see a squirrel rifle, a corncob pipe, or a dogrun shanty. Much of this stuff was absolute trash, but some of it was not. Good or bad, it was popular and from the point of view of folklorists of the

*** On the other hand, during the long Musicians Union strike in the Thirties it was necessary for radio to use material in the public domain.**

strict interpretation it irremediably corrupted the authentic voice of the folk.

What happened as a matter of fact was that the commercial exploitation of hillbilly songs coincided with the collapse of the marginal small farm in the South, the great droughts of the Dust Bowl, the World Economic Crisis, and the migration of the people of the Southern Hills to California and the big cities of the North. Out of this change of background developed the city-billy song. Folk singers of the Southern hills had the deepest roots in their environment of any people in America. Not only their songs, but their ways of life, went back to the Middle Ages in Great Britain. In the sharpest possible contrast the characteristic of the city-billy is that he is uprooted, in an environment that shatters all of his old interpersonal relationships. It is certainly impossible for a descendant of the people in Sir Walter Scott's novels to sink roots in the sidewalks of Chicago's West Madison Street. The city-billy was a displaced person, just like the youth of Paris in 1946. A new kind of sorrow comes into the music. The lyrics tell of broken marriages, poverty, homesickness, dislocation, and a refusal to accept the so-called middle-class values of the Northern cities, and the sexual ethics of respectable people. It is out of this background, not from the old world of the isolated valleys of subsistence farmers, with singers entertaining the folks in a country store, that Elvis Presley comes. It is Elvis Presley who established folk rock in its worldwide popularity. Presley's lyrics may be commercialized and sentimentalized in large part but they too are alienated. Even at his most hackneyed he speaks from outside the dominant culture. Like James Dean he was the physical type of the displaced youth created by our new technological society. All that was necessary during the next ten years was to improve technically his medium, get rid of the bad taste and commercialism, develop the music, and make every effort to keep the lyrics honest and at the same time use the words and music to push against the old patterns of thought towards a new sensibility that would be, by its very nature, unassimilable by the dominant culture and able to stand on its own. This is what happened. Elvis Presley was only one of several. They were all "show business" and capable of immensely profitable exploitation, but if it had not been for the craze they created it would have been far more difficult for their successors to overtake and surpass them. Business enterprise had opened a Pandora's Box.

There was plenty in the box. All sorts of things had come together in the middle Fifties to form the chemical compound of a new, genuinely popular music. Radio and television with their all-consuming demand had destroyed the commercial pop tune. There would never be another *Trail of the Lonesome Pine* or *Three O'Clock in the Morning*. In fact, the most popular song programs with more sophisticated young people were precisely the revivals—"Hit Parades of 1900–1935." Jazz had given up melody, lyrics, and dance rhythm. It would be possible to dance to the hard bop bands that played the Five Spot or even to Charles Mingus but only if you were Martha Graham or Pearl Primus. Melodies were chosen solely because of the harmonic structure of the melodic lines, if it lent itself to "changes"—development in chords and arpeggios. The modern jazz musicians of the Fifties were interested primarily in using these materials as exhibitions of virtuosity in solos. Each man took a chorus and the ensemble receded into the background. Most of the tunes were show tunes of the most vulgar, commercial sort, chosen simply because they were harmonically the slickest. The lyrics were embarrassingly commercialized sentimentality. Only a Frank Sinatra or an Ella Fitzgerald could make them believable and these two singers, because they swing, are also the only two that all modern jazz musicians liked. Most singers were simply resented as an unpleasantness forced on the band by the club owner and the nightclub audience. Had the leading jazz musicians of the Fifties worked with the folk and protest singers who were coming up in those days, they would not have lost, almost totally, their youthful white audience. Had they not been so violently opposed to the insistent beat of the rhythm and blues, soon to be called "rock and roll," dance bands, and if they had not rejected the gutsy lyrics of the rhythm and blues singers, they would not have lost their black audience. Dinah Washington was put down as corny by the same musicians who tirelessly played Stan Getz's embroidery of *Autumn Leaves*. This was the McCarthy epoch—the other McCarthy—and the voice of youth was largely confined to science fiction and the folk and protest singers. People who had come up first in the Depression like Pete Seeger and Woody Guthrie were more popular with militantly anti-political students than they had been in the heyday of Café Society Downtown and Café Society Uptown, the expensive *boîtes* of the upwardly mobile (headed for the executive suites on Madison Avenue) Left intelligentsia of the old days. If young people wanted to dance they tuned in the black rock-and-roll stations with their commercials every sixty seconds. "A dollar down and a dollar a day," as the song says. One of the most important things about this music is that the lyrics reflected an entirely different kind of life from that depicted by the country blues or city blues of the previous generation, a life that was uprooted and fierce, in which love relationships were entirely different than those of the prostitutes' songs like *St. Louis Blues* or *Easy Rider,* deeper, richer, and yet even more fragile. It was out of this kind of love song or the city-billy laments over lost lovers and broken marriages and the brief times of happiness that the new white love lyric of the present was to grow. Johnny Ace's *My Song* with its strange broken back rhythm and Japanese tonality anticipated both Donovan and Joni Mitchell or Judy Collins or Françoise Hardy. Johnny Ace, alas, was confined to the black nightclub and lodge dances of the Southwest and killed himself playing Russian Roulette on a stage in Dallas before the horrified eyes of the sweetheart he was trying to impress. Fats Domino or Ray Charles hung on to win finally a vast and integrated acceptance. Most of the girl singers wore out early. The modern hard blues of the hard core of the big cities was a kind of protest song of its own, but most of these singers are men still unknown to white musicians, and their only discernible influence on the youngest musicians I know is on the Southern California group now disbanded, "The United States of America." It is significant that "U.S.A." are all sophisticated intellectuals. Country Joe and the Fish derive from older styles of raw blues, mostly of the Southwest style, and from the *I.W.W. Little Red Song Book.*

Suddenly Tin Pan Alley woke up and began to cover black rock with a thick coat of whitewash. No sooner would a Fats Domino or Little Richard record hit the top ten on the juke boxes in the ghetto bars and barbecue joints than a manufactured imitation rolled off the presses for the bobby sox drive-in trade. The only trouble was that the best rock singers pushed their way up past their white imitators and began to create their own white audience. Essential to their appeal was not only the roll and bump music which was perfect for open and highly figured dancing then popular—"jitterbugging" the squares still called it—but the lyrics which spoke for a world opted out by very definition. Young men and women sitting late at night in a ghetto barbecue eating ribs, red beans, and chitlins and listening to Floyd Price's *Lawdy, Lawdy, Lawdy Miss Claudie* or *Blue Suede Shoes* did not need to sport beads, bedspread ponchos, whiskers, or bare feet, like signs around their necks saying "I am alienated." That was apparent at a glance. Elvis's *Blue Suede Shoes* was a runaway hit, but those were shoes on white feet. Elvis's *Hound Dog* and *Heartbreak Hotel* derived directly from rhythm-and-blues songs and differed primarily in their city-billy sentimentality, an ingredient which was sprinkled liberally over almost all city-billy music at the insistence of the music business. The black audiences for the originals rejected sentimentality. They couldn't afford it. The sentimental black man has a hard time surviving.

Nevertheless Elvis was the first singer of the type to gain large audiences from all classes and ages. His popularity was more widely spread than even Frank Sinatra. It coincided with the last days of bop, and the growing popularity of Thelonius Monk, Pacific Jazz, and New York hard bop. At this point there occurred a schism between jazz musicians and rhythm and blues, later rock and roll, and the folk singers, real and pseudo, that has never been healed. The most advanced jazz musicians not only detested Elvis, but Woody Guthrie and Fats Domino as well. Most jazz was based on show tunes, the same things popularized by the cocktail pianists and Lawrence Welk or Mantovani. The reason for this was musical; the chord progressions lent themselves to the rather simpleminded dissonances of the long-drawn-out theme and variations of bop solos. Having made this choice, jazz unwittingly cut itself loose from a youthful audience, and as the years have gone by, has steadily declined in popularity while, at the same time, pricing itself out of the market. Today the record sales of any one top rock group are greater than those of all jazz musicians put together and there is only a handful of clubs left in the United States where serious jazz musicians can play the kind of music they want—to an audience whose grey hairs increase noticeably at each tour.

We are at the breakthrough point. Folk music is about to sweep everything before it. What makes it folk? Not its appearance in collections of Scotch border and Southern hill ballads gathered by academic folklorists, certainly. I suppose folk song is distinguished by its natural expression of an organic community. Commercial pop music is a manufactured commodity produced by people for whom what it purports to express has little or no personal meaning—"June, moon, spoon." Who believes it? Yet the music business was instinctively searching for a connection with a new audience. The calypso fad was an abortive attempt to capture the new taste. There were several things wrong with that. In the first place calypso was simply exotic. The problems and values of a West Indian Negro are almost as remote as those of a Hawaiian sugar-cane worker. Just like the long ago Hawaiian craze, calypso soon became synthetic and pitched at a white café audience. What carried the popularity of calypso was its use as dance music along with Latin bands like Perez Prado's and the skill and infectious audience personality of a few great singers like Harry Belafonte. For my taste, Belafonte is better as a moderately concertized folk singer with a diversified repertory than in calypso. Belafonte was the last expression of the old Café Society Downtown—Uptown folklorism for the Left liberal audiences of New York—Pete Seeger, Woody Guthrie, Billie Holiday. Belafonte has always had the good taste to avoid the commodities manufactured for this audience, the most famous of which undoubtedly was Billie Holiday's *Strange Fruit,* moving doubtless to its white Northern audience but so synthetic that it would have been met with baffled incomprehension if sung in a bar on Chicago's South Side or in the Dallas ghetto, or Pete Seeger's equally synthetic *I Dreamed I Saw Joe Hill Last Night*. It was this type of cooked "voice of the common people" that effectively limited Pete Seeger's appeal and to a lesser degree Guthrie's. Today they are still influential to the degree that they drop overt political pamphlets from their repertory. Guthrie of course is dead, and his son Arlo is far less political.

A big factor in laying the foundations of the folklore edifice was actual public presentation of folkloristic work. Songs appeared on radio that had been collected in the field all over the world. The folklore collections of the Library of Congress are immense. Folkways Records has reproduced the songs of almost every known source, from primitive tribes to the occupational songs of fraternity boys, railroaders, and stevedores. This stuff didn't get a mass audience but it certainly got a large one, especially amongst students, and it was broadcast by stations like WGNY and WBAI in New York and KPFA and KPFK on the West Coast, and sung in innumerable student parties.

Stamped with the lion and the unicorn and marked "purveyors by Special Appointment to the Royal Family," The Beatles and The Rolling Stones suddenly made roll and bump respectable. Before they hoved on the scene no white musician and no self-respecting black musician, instrumentalists and singers alike, would have been caught dead listening to the stuff spun by the disk jockeys on the dollar-down dollar-a-day black stations. It was quite impossible to get any jazz musician to enter a roll-and-bump club to listen. If he was short of bread and had to take such a gig to stay alive, he bitched about it *ad nauseam*. What they objected to was the sock, the overpowering simple beat, and the primitive chord structures. The extraordinary instrumental and vocal gymnastics left them unimpressed. To make a guitar wail like a soprano saxophone blown by somebody with gigantic lungs or to make the human voice like an autobus boring through the desert night was detested as the worst kind of corn. It is interesting that these effects all had the wail that was soon to be taken up and excelled by electronic devices. It's hard to say why the lyrics of the rock and roll or the contemporary Chicago city blues were so disliked. Probably they were just too down-home and the jazz musicians of the Fifties came from middle-class black families with no connection with the deepest recesses of the ghetto, much less the country. It was ten years before the disciples of Webern and Stockhausen on the stand in the Five Spot would discover that "black is beautiful"; LeRoi Jones in those days was a Zen Buddhist and loved all sentient creatures. Always bear in mind that anybody almost anywhere in America at any hour of the day or night by the flip of a dial can turn on the voice of Blackness, the actual interpersonal communication of the walled ghetto. Older people were listening to Turk Murphy or Charles Mingus or Jimmy Guifre and to Frank Sinatra and Ella Fitzgerald, when people in high school began to disturb their parents with "rock and roll." It is interesting that the heyday of rhythm and blues, rock and roll, was from the end of the war to about 1952. White kids started to listen to it only after it had entered its decline and become commercialized. Commercialized or no, it was quite impossible to hold its own audience unless the lyrics spoke in their terms and for their values. These lay totally outside the dominant culture and were antagonistic to it all along the line. The effect on white youth, alienated by the constant threat of death in a succession of wars to which they could see no end except universal extinction, was as galvanic as an electric shock.

All this accumulated musical expression, antagonistic to the music business, constituted a tremendous head of steam piled up and ready to blow. Along came The Beatles, overtaking in popularity at the very outset their then slightly better rivals, The Rolling Stones. They were white. They were English and might someday get knighthoods or at least C.B.E.'s. They were cute, they were cuddly, and their Liverpuddlean accents were hilarious. Their lyrics were studded with remarks in code which, if understood, would have horrified Papa and Mama. Not least, John Lennon and Paul McCartney had considerable talent as poets. Even their literary amateurishness added to their charm. They took the sentiments, they took the rhythms, of black rhythm and blues, accentuated the role and bump, applied a thin coat of whitewash. Their distortion of the specific swing of rhythm and blues had a faintly comic exotic charm rather like k'oto and samisen renditions of Bach's *Well-Tempered Clavichord* with Oriental phrasing and ornamentation. Everybody went wild. The breakthrough had occurred. Within a couple of years John Lennon was perfectly right when he said, "We have more influence than Jesus Christ." Although editorial writers all over the world blew up at this remark, it really reflected The Beatles' awareness of their frightening responsibilities and they began to "mature." Each year of course they grew older, and at the time of life, the end of adolescence, when every six months counts. They not only came to take their enormous influence seriously. It dogged them and worried them constantly. They were always under a pressure of conscience to live up to it. They were the first to face the problem that confronts all their English and American successors, and that had been with the French singers like Brassens, Ferré, Piaf, Greco for twenty years. If you can make a million defying the Establishment, how do you escape corruption? It's not just that you're going to be bought out. You are going to find yourself living a kind of life that is incompatible with any profound defiance. You always are tempted to become a kept rebel and an allowed clown. Whether Allen Ginsberg, The Beatles, Bob Dylan, Leonard Cohen, The Jefferson Airplane, The Mothers of Invention—this is the problem which all the spokesmen of the counter-culture must face every minute—cooptation.

Perhaps the most significant thing about The Beatles was that they were more assimilable internationally than the singers from whom they have come. A blues singer on the Southwest circuit or an American Left protest singer in Café Society Downtown was remote from the interests of all but small groups in Italy, Sweden, Japan, or India. The Beatles reduced their sources to a common denominator that could be negotiated anywhere that modern Western civilization could spread and many places that it had not. For instance, at first The Beatles were unfamiliar with the High Life music and song of English-speaking black Africa, but there is a remarkable similarity in even their earliest pieces.

The folklore movement, partly scholarly, partly social in inspiration, but certainly as square as could well be, burst its confines at about the same time and suddenly became an international expression of the counter-culture. Joan Baez was soon able to command audiences almost as big as those of The Beatles, although her repertory was largely traditional English and American folk song. It is interesting that her sister and brother-in-law Mimi and Richard Fariña were amongst the very first of the new generation with its own new folklore. Their repertory gave expression to a new set of values, a new way of life which, so short a time ago, commanded very large audiences. Fariña died, but today he is unknown to the very young who listen to The

Doors or The Serpent Power, and is remembered by connoisseurs in their twenties whom the mass audience considers already middle-aged. (Recently the Fariñas have been rediscovered.)

Before we conclude this survey it is essential to understand that although one kind of explanation can show the evolution from within of public poetry as the return to the relationships of pre-literate literature, the determining factors were external. These are the years of the final breakdown of a civilization. It broke down in August 1914, never to be repaired, but it still functioned in a dangerous patched-up fashion. In the years since the Second War, Western civilization has ceased to exist. We live in a corpse which jerks like a dead frog on a hot wire. All the many symptoms of total breakdown have entered into and determined the content and course of poetry and song. It is a mistake to talk about protest songs, protest poetry. Protest assumes a possibility for correction. It occurs from within a culture. As the long tale of horror has gone by, protest has changed to alienation, alienation to total secession. The war is permanent. Only battlefields and casualties change. The racial conflicts raging, not just in America, but in dozens of countries around the world, are irreducible within any existing social system. The sexual morality of puritanical Moscow and Peking, of debauched Cairo, of the cocktail lounges of Manhattan, of sex-carnival Copenhagen, is absurd, intolerable, soul-destroying, and however it may differ in its symptoms, it is everywhere the same world ill. The acquisitive society, the business ethic, is as unacceptable in Tokyo or Moscow as it is in Chicago. The galvanic twitchings of a dead civilization are not minor tremors but terrible spasms that kill everything in the neighborhood. Each stage in the escalation of death, the Vietnam War, race riots, the poison gassing of whole universities, effects directly and immediately the poetic expression of the counter-culture, and on the other hand, the dead men are always there with their check books—"accentuate the upbeat," ready for cooptation. Most of the rock groups and folk singers have now gone wholesome, and others, faced with commercialization by agents and record companies, have dissolved.

It is the coherence of the counter-culture, its spiritual independence of the dominant society, given its final shape by the worldwide revulsion against the Vietnam War, which accounts for the sudden proliferation of the same kind of cultural expression, the raising of the same voices everywhere. It's not that Joan Baez or The Beatles or Bob Dylan have thousands of imitators. Wolf Biermann in East Berlin, Barbara in Paris, Fred Åkerström and Cornelis Vreeswijk in Sweden, Ryoko Moriyama in Japan—it's all the same universe of discourse, because it's all the same audience listening to the same spokesmen speaking against the same evil and for the same good. To put it fatuously, "it's a whole new self-contained system of values."

This is why it is so difficult to talk about the present situation. There's just too much, so it's a matter of largely stylistic taste. Some prefer hard blues, some prefer James Brown, some prefer Simon and Garfunkel, some prefer the direct protest of Country Joe and the Fish. On the whole my own taste runs to poet singers who get to the root of the matter, who speak for fundamental changes in the sensibility in human relationships and therefore in language. Dylan at his best, Donovan, Leonard Cohen, Joni Mitchell, Judy Collins when she sings her own things—there are countless people like this all over the world, more perhaps in France than elsewhere. Much of the entertainment that went on night and day in the Theatre Odéon during the 1968 May revolt had nothing overtly to do with the, after all passing, revolt in the streets, the evils of the regime, or the betrayals of the political Left. People sang songs that attacked the evil at its source by presenting an alternative kind of human being.

America which leads the world musically because of the Blacks, lags far behind in the relationship of "real poets," poets of print to poets of song, in spite of the tremendous popularity of poetry readings. There is a record of Joan Baez singing a wide variety of people from Henry Treece to my own translations of the Japanese, but that's almost all. Nobody sings Ginsberg, Patchen, or Ferlinghetti, all eminently singable. Nobody even sings Lenore Kandel, which is hard to believe. Partly this is due to inexpertise of composers. Only the straight musicians seem to know how to put free verse to music. Over the years I have accumulated dozens of tapes and scores of my own poems sent me by composers, but their public performance has been extremely limited. I suppose this is true of other poets as well. The poets themselves almost never know anything about music, even jazz or rock, they just "dig" it. David Meltzer, one of the San Francisco group, is the only person I know who is both a literary poet and a writer and singer, with his wife Tina, of his own poems. For this reason his two records, *Serpent Power* and *Poet Sing,* are most significant. This way lies the future, assuming that other people who are at once good poets, performers, and composers turn up.

In the days when I used to do poetry-and-jazz I was astonished to discover that hardly any American poetry could be projected to an audience in a jazz club. This was true even of Vachel Lindsay, who thought that was precisely what he was doing. The best were very early Carl Sandburg, Kenneth Patchen, some love poems of Muriel Ruykeyser, and Langston Hughes. Mostly when I got tired of my own stuff I translated from the French—Carco, Queneau, Seghers, Bruant, Appollinaire. This discovery did more than anything else to wake me up to a fundamental flaw in the American relationship of poet and audience and therefore in the poetry itself. You can project the French god of America's literary poets, Paul Valéry, whether in French or English, but you can't project them themselves.

The largest body of poetic input of high quality in contemporary people poetry is Negro song, blues and spiritual. The poetic value, the esthetic power, of even commercialized rhythm and blues is extraordinarily high, and the lyrics of standard classic blues or spirituals are very great poetry indeed. This cannot be assimilated directly. For one thing the emotional manipulation of repetition is special to Negro song, American, Caribbean, or African, so much so that it is almost an instinctive skill. With it goes the shifting of accents and quantity, the seemingly irrational emphasis or lengthening of syllables, which few white people can imitate and which most of them don't even know is happening. So the immensely popular British "blues revival" doesn't quite come off. The things sound monotonous or hysterical. When the repetitions are cut out, as on the record of the group The United States of America, the lyrics tend to seem flat and empty—although not always. This is why the most fruitful source so far has been what the singers call country and western, actually city-billy, derived from the traditional melodies of the ancient English and Scottish ballads and Irish folk song. This is as true of Leonard Cohen as it is of Johnny Cash. It's not a question of copying. The rhythms of a people's folk song are so permanent you might almost believe they came with the DNA.

1969

14.
Poetry into the '70's

Five years ago I wrote a survey of American poetry by poets under thirty-five and followed it with a piece on the economics of the craft, how poets live, and if, how, and why publishers publish poetry. There have been great changes since. It is time to bring things up to date. Most everything I said has to be modified and in some cases is no longer true at all. Most of the prophecies, however, turned out to be correct.

If poetry plays the social role of a symbolic criticism of values, it is hardly surprising that American poetry should have been productive and undergone great changes in the past five years. We are in the midst of a time of wholesale overturn, a transvaluation of values at least comparable to the revolutionary years around 1848, if not to the time of the invention of pottery and agriculture, weaving and herding, or the time when men first began to live in cities. This brief period has been one of proliferating social conflicts which have spread to the most remote corners of the world. The generation gap in America has become a fearsome chasm. The race problem in America is believed by ever increasing numbers of intelligent people, black and white, to be insoluble within the context of the present culture. The battles of the common people of both races threaten to destroy our cities. Over all has loomed the horror of the Vietnam War, which has destroyed, not just the American system of protective alliances, but the very memory of America's moral leadership.

Man's relationship to his environment has broken down, and cool-headed scientists go about saying that the human species may be extinct by the end of the century. Ecological catastrophe has struck everywhere. Los Angeles, Paris, Milan, New York smother under a blanket of carcinogens. In the old refuges of the world-weary—Bali, the South Sea Islands, the jungles of Africa and Asia—swarming populations starve on exhausted soil. At both ends of the teetering ladder of civilization, men battle each other for irrational objectives. What is surprising is that American poetry is not more crisis-ridden, that some people are still able to recollect their emotions in tranquillity, are still writing *Tintern Abbeys* and *Dover Beaches.*

America may lead, like Virgil leading Dante through the Inferno, in the crisis of values, but it is everywhere, and the universalization of the present human condition has led to the internationalization of American poetry to a degree that it has never known before. There are benign reasons for this as well—the "prosperity" of the metropoles, the ease and rapidity of communication, the electronic technology. The youth culture is now completely international. As it swings into the future, one of its hinges is poetry—the other is music. The third is drugs, a prosthesis to keep the door from collapsing altogether.

Life in the East Village, the Haight-Ashbury, Notting Hill, Shinjuku, Kings Cross, Schwabing, is not just of one pattern; it is no longer necessary to understand even a few words of the different languages, and in the far-away caravanserais on the Great Grass Road, in Kabul, or Katmandu, people communicate in a sub-verbal Esperanto. Wandering youth from all over the world, always with a surprisingly large band of angry Americans, can be found in Vietnam demonstrations in Trafalgar Square, the Place de la Concorde, and Mexico City's Avenida de la Reforma.

Outside their own country Allen Ginsberg, Andrei Voznesensky, Gary Snyder, draw audiences as large as Jacques Brel, Wolf Biermann, or Joan Baez, audiences who don't need a dictionary to know what they say. The largest poetry concert I've ever given was in Tokyo. They had to put public address speakers out in the street. The same thing happened to Voznesensky in the old Fillmore Auditorium, which must have had a capacity of 2500. In both instances the audience shouted down the translators.

It's quite a shock to turn from this scene, with its passionate sense of community and its turmoil and conflict with the dominant society, to the still lingering world of conventional poetry. The classic American modernists—Eliot, Pound, William Carlos Williams, Marianne Moore, Wallace Stevens—have become the idols of academia, something like those empty chairs back of the pulpit in Protestant churches that little children think are for the Trinity, obsolete Molochs to which the babies refuse to be fed. All you have to do is to get away from the big-time, big-city schools, and into the provinces, to discover that they are still being taught as "contemporary poets." The reason is obvious. They are God's own gift to literary Alexandrians. Explication of their texts can go on forever and get nowhere. Teaching them is as quiet and profitable as the specialty of dermatology; as the skin men say, "the patient never gets cured and never dies." Courses of this kind have probably quadrupled in the past five years. Academia is up to its eyebrows in poetasters-in-residence.

My own generation is now entering the home stretch of collected editions—Kenneth Patchen, Muriel Rukeyser, Elizabeth Bishop, Babette Deutsch, Richard Eberhart, Theodore Roethke, Randall Jarrell, Delmore Schwartz, Robert Lowell, Richard Wilbur. We are not just the Establishment—some are dead; the rest of us are the oldest living poets, except Pound and Marianne Moore, who no longer write. Few reputations have survived from the Post-War I years—collected editions of Malcolm Cowley and Yvor Winters have come out and re-established them as leading "younger poets" of those years.

With the exception of Allen Ginsberg, the graying post-War II avant-garde is also thoroughly assimilated and its members are now the subject of explications of text themselves. One by one in the next five years they will be slinking into the National Institute of Arts and Letters where they will be indistinguishable from everybody else. In preparation, some of my best friends are giving up grass and taking to cocktails and nicotine.

Denise Levertov, Robert Bly, Galway Kinnell, and Allen Ginsberg, amongst others, have been very active leaders of the poetic protest against the war. Lawrence Ferlinghetti has written several overtly and specifically political poems, far better than the ones that were written in the proletarian Thirties, but the best poem directed specifically against the Vietnam War, folly by folly, and horror by horror, is by Robert Bly, a long nightmare sermon, the *Lay of Maldoror* come true. The Vietnam poetry read-ins which have been held on campuses all over the country have attracted immense audiences of both young and old and have drawn in as participants most of the leading poets of each region. These vast affairs have brought many older poets closer to the counter-culture, which many of them didn't even know existed, and given them enthusiastic appreciation amongst young people who didn't know *they* existed.

It's illuminating to participate in these read-ins on college campuses. The metaphor "separating the sheep from the goats" is only too apt. The creative-poetry, teaching-seven-types-of-ambiguity, literary-quarterly types don't participate; they don't even come, although they are most anxious to be invited to, or even to stage, cocktail parties for the celebrities.

The prize students in courses in creative writing graduate to the various poetry series. The number of these has greatly increased, but they remain almost totally impenetrable to the counter-culture. They are still given over to little Wallace Stevenses, William Carlos Williamses, and alas, even little Rexroths, with here and there a junior Creeley carefully self-explicating himself. It's over fifteen years since *Howl,* but no little Ginsbergs or little Ferlinghettis get into these poetry series, even when a person like Denise Levertov, one of the Post-War II avant-garde, is an editor. Yet these things are not all bad. They keep little minds from mischief and once in a while a good poet slips by. After all it has not yet become totally impossible to write book poetry. Sometimes a fresh editor or a fresh project will produce somebody remarkable indeed. Wesleyan, Indiana, Pitt, Columbia, Washington, Atheneum, Grossman, Appleton Century Croft, Alan Swallow, Penguin, Louisiana, Cornell, Rutgers, all publish regular poetry series of several books a year. Some of them also import similar series from England. The larger trade publishers are far more hospitable to poetry than they were five years ago. Harper & Row, Doubleday, Simon and Schuster, Farrar, Straus and Giroux, Harcourt, Holt, Rinehart and Winston, Oxford, Houghton Mifflin, Norton, Barnes, Bobbs Merrill—every one of these publishers has brought out some poetry recently, sometimes several titles. The most ambitious series is Wesleyan, and in the last five years it has first published ten new poets of whom Michael Benedikt and John Haines are real discoveries, as well as new books by Robert Bly, James Wright, Philip Levine, James Dickey, Josephine Miles, David Ignatow. This is just a sample of what a small university press, none too rich, can accomplish. The University of California Press, smack in the heart of the action, is aggressively uninterested in contemporary poets. Columbia University Press recently inaugurated such a program and soon turned up a very exciting and thoroughly contemporary poet, Joseph Ceravolo. For my taste he would even be more exciting if he were sung by Simon and Garfunkel or Joan Baez.

This is where it's at. In France poetry left the printed page twenty-five years ago. The leading post-war French poets are Georges Brassens, Anne Sylvestre, Barbara, Jacques Brel. The good literary poets of the past are all sung. The best of the present ones write deliberately to be sung. In the English-speaking world things move slowly. Bob Dylan, Paul McCartney and John Lennon, Donovan, Simon and Garfunkel, Richard Fariña, and others are significant and certainly stimulating, but they are still vastly uneven. Donovan, Dylan, and Fariña are certainly amongst the most important poets, even if sometimes they do sound like collaborations of Rimbaud and Ella Wheeler Wilcox, André Breton, and Lawrence Hope. The puzzling thing is that nobody sings Ginsberg or Ferlinghetti, although you can hear similar French poets—Pierre MacOrlan,

Raymond Queneau, Jacques Prévert, Pierre Seghers, in Parisian *cafés chantants* any night in the week, and there are thirty-four different melodies recorded for Apollinaire's *Pont Mirabeau.* Gary Snyder, Philip Whalen, and a number of younger people who have been closely associated with music are even more singable. Lenore Kandel knows at least 90 per cent of the rock musicians on the San Francisco scene. Why on earth don't they put her to music? With a good voice and a good group she'd be in the top 40 if not the top 10. The most significant poet to become popular as a singer since Bob Dylan is Leonard Cohen. He already had a tremendous reputation amongst young people in Canada, but he was unknown in America before his first record, where his reputation was largely confined to his colleagues. I never met anyone who had heard of him except Ginsberg, Ferlinghetti, and Dylan. People are still saying to this day that he has been influenced by Dylan, when of course it's the other way around and it is Leonard Cohen's example which accounts for the increasing magic, order, and depth in Dylan's own words. He may well be the greatest poet Canada has ever produced in English. He is certainly Canada's first international writer. It is significant that he is the only English-Canadian poet familiar with young modernist French Canadian poets. The three leading Canadian poets of my own generation spend all the time they can get off from teaching jobs in France, and yet are oblivious to the French poetry written in their own country. Not so Leonard Cohen, which may be a minor reason why he is the first major poet turned singer on this side of the Atlantic. Comparisons are stuffy, but he is probably a little better than Georges Brassens and quite the equal of the singer Anne Sylvestre, the most important woman poet in France in a long, long time, and he is considerably better than Wolf Biermann.

On First Looking into Chapman's Homer—the impact of Leonard Cohen is one of those completely novel poetic experiences, like first reading Baudelaire's *La Cloche fêlée,* or Rimbaud's *Le Bateau ivre,* in early youth, and there's not many people going around who can do that. With the exception of Dylan, Joni Mitchell, and Judy Collins (when she sings her own songs), and the late Richard Fariña, there's nobody else in America who is writing really important poetry and singing it who is getting heard except, recently, David Meltzer, one of the San Francisco group, who has three very impressive records, *The Serpent Power, Poet Sing,* and *Let the Light Shine In.* This is the future; it's all about us in the present college generation. I conduct a class called "Poetry and Song" at the University of California, Santa Barbara, where people write and sing their own things, and the talent continuously amazes me. The atmosphere is a combination of the first years of the hungry i, the Fillmore Auditorium, Soulville, and an underground mass—*agape* everywhere, and all the time is show time; the students are endlessly fecund with songs, poems, and music. This is what people want to do, the blossom and fruit of the counterculture, and the contrast with dehydrated "creative poetry" produce is even more amazing.

Out of the great forests of the Pacific Northwest, out of the communal tradition of the I.W.W. and Kropotkin's *Mutual Aid,* Gary Snyder was the poetic voice of the ecological revolution twelve years before anybody else had ever heard the term. Fresh out of Reed College he and Philip Whalen were talking about such outlandish ideas as an ecological esthetics and prosody and the Buddha's command to respect all living beings. Today, as the dominant society goes down trapped in its own filth, like quicksand, ecology has become a desperate fashion, and the youth revolt, the alternative society, has raised the slogan, "Down with the Red Flag! Down with the Black Flag! Up with the Green!" It is not surprising that Snyder and Whalen, with Allen Ginsberg who turns up once again like a shiny gold piece rather than like a bad penny, have become, as poets, the most influential spokesmen, or even ideologists, of a new and revolutionary system of values, based on a constant, prayerful sense of the interlocking responsibilties of the community of all life on earth.

The greatest change in five years has been in American Negro poetry. During the early years of the Post-War II civil rights struggle and the succeeding increase in education and skilled and white-collar employment for Negroes there was a decided slump in literary output. Back in the days of the Harlem Renaissance, "When the Negro was in Vogue" as Langston Hughes said, all a sensitive and well-educated Negro could do was write poems or novels. From 1955 to 1965 most educated Black people were too busy. Even James Baldwin, a writer who had always fought shy of being a "race man," became an impassioned spokesman of the struggle. During the last five years, for better or worse, the juridically defined objectives have mostly been obtained and been found wanting. The younger generation of the Black urban middle class has been permitted to take part in some of the benefits of the affluent society. In many universities the number of Black students had increased tenfold or more.

The counter-culture always welcomes the Negro. Countee Cullen, Claude MacKay, and Langston Hughes were completely accepted in the social world of *Masses* and *New Masses* readers and contributors. Norman Mailer called the beatnik "the white Negro," although the typical Beats saw only their own chauvinistic stereotypes in their Black friends. In the past five years large numbers of young Negro intellectuals have first entered the alternative society, rejecting the values of both the white and Black middle classes, and then in turn have withdrawn from the secession of white youth into a militant *negritude* of their own. Their most famous spokesman has been LeRoi Jones, whose poems have become almost entirely insults and incitements hurled at the white race. At the moment he is conducting a synthetic Africanist ashram, which has been greeted with hoots of scornful laughter by both Black Muslims and Black Africans. Nevertheless, romantic Africanism does represent a kind of magical attempt to exorcise the much mooted "identity crisis" of the American Negro intellectual. This transitory phase of militant negritude naturally finds expression in poetry. The best work has been gathered by LeRoi Jones and Larry Neal in a substantial anthology, *Black Fire*. Jones's hymns to the delights of missionary soup are amusing. What is unforgivable is his vicious anti-Semitism, far worse than Ezra Pound's ever was. It is interesting that, for all their militant Black nationalism, most of the poets in the book show little sensitivity to the rhythms of Negro song or even speech, whether African or Black American. The test is simple. Give the book to a good Black blues singer and have the poems read aloud. Something is missing. This is not true of some of the people and they are the best in the book.

There are plenty of young Black writers around who say, "What identity crisis?" Some of them are assimilated to the dominant culture and insist on being published simply as poets. Gloria Oden for years submitted her poetry as by G. C. Oden and never provided editors with information about either her race or her sex, a sure way to discover if you're being published on your own merits. The Black poets in Paul Carroll's anthology, Alden Van Buskirk, Gerald William Barrax, were chosen because they wrote good poems, not because they were Black, and they are amongst the best in the book. One of the problems, as Harold Cruse points out in his book *The Crisis of the Negro Intellectual,* is the tendency of Black intellectuals to form very exclusive cliques—so the best way to discover what is happening is to read through *all* the anthologies of Black writing, of which there are a half dozen or more in print. It is interesting to contrast them with the collections of African writing which is so much harder, clearer, and more self-confident. This is especially true of Black South Africans, who certainly suffer from more disabilities than Black Americans. However riven by struggles, internal and external, distorted by fads, misled by masochistic white claques, the new poetry of young American Negroes is still one of the most exciting developments in recent years and some of these people are surely amongst the very best poets to appear in this time, of whatever color.

When I lecture at colleges people are always asking me, "What about concrete poetry?" Well, what about it? When you've seen one redwood tree, you've seen them all. I have followed the development of concrete poetry since its revival in Brazil and the Rhineland, and dutifully read all the publications. Like electronic music, with which the leaders are closely associated, concrete poetry is still extremely primitive and belongs in large-scale intermedia productions rather than on the printed page. Aram Saroyan, Augusto and Haroldo de Campos, Max Bense, Ian Hamilton Finlay, would all be more effective if the words were projected on walls and ceiling in the midst of a clavilux light show, to the accompaniment of moog music, while voices in the audience shouted or warbled counterpointing words. On the printed page concrete poetry tends to be just little bits of typographical humor. It is far, far, from having produced a Homer or even a Bashō. Max Bense and the de Campos brothers are also very interested in computer poetry, I don't think computers are likely to ever write the works of Shakespeare. Those ten billion monkeys hitting typewriters at random never did. But the computer poetry I have seen has almost all of it been very good stuff for poets to read, especially aloud, because it opens up new ways of meaning, new syntaxes of the sensibility, and new extended rhythms—ragas of words. It's the latter we need to discover how to program, rather than leave to accident. We should be able to feed the machine series that are steadily evolving rhythmic sequences like the prime numbers, 3.1416, or the Napierian logarithmic base, or the square root of 1, translated into sound of words, and see what happens. Nobody has done this yet and since the elements which can now be analyzed out of speech by sound spectographs and other phonetic apparatus are exceedingly complex, this is not going to be easy to do, but it needs doing. Max Bense envisages a development of a completely scientific prosody, something of course which does not exist at all at present. One of the best things about the concrete-poetry movement is its complete internationalism. Everybody knows everybody else, and they're all terribly excited about what each person is doing. This is all to the good, another move towards the complete internationalization of post-modern culture. Most people have an idea that the concrete poets are weird superhippy types. Nothing could be less true. Most of them are very much Herr Doktor Wissenschaft, conservatively dressed technicians, veritable Mies Van Der Rohe's of the printed word. After all, it is precisely in the Bauhaus and revolutionary Russia that concrete poetry was born, long, long ago, to be forgotten for two generations.

The biggest change in thc past five years has been economic. Publishers have discovered that if they hire poetry editors who know what they are doing, then poetry is profitable. Anthologies like Paul Carroll's sell like hotcakes and anything by or about Negro poetry has the immediate market of the innumerable Black culture courses now so fashionable in the colleges. Leonard Cohen's *Selected Poems* received little promotion from his U.S. publishers. They must have been dumbfounded when he appeared in the picture magazines and *Suzanne* became the first genuinely popular song in a generation —recalling the days of *The Trail of the Lonesome Pine* or *Pretty Baby.* Philip Whalen's collected poems, *On Bear's Head,* in the hardcover edition was one of the highest priced trade books of poetry ever published. Poets picketed the publisher in protest, yet the book sold, and now in cheap paperback sells very well. Some of the poets in the various poetry series are published in editions of 5000 or less and these are immediately snapped up by bookdealers, especially those who sell to university libraries. As one of them said to me, "Any book of poetry which isn't complete vanity publication trash will double in price three years after it goes off the market." Thinking this over I believe it is probably the most significant statement possible on the contemporary market for poetry.

Underneath the world of trade publishing, mimeographed, fugitively printed, or duplicated books, poetry readings, little magazines, have proliferated beyond all bounds. Every city of any size has its Haight-Ashbury and its underground press. From London's *It* to Milwaukee's *Kaleidoscope* they all print poetry. Most of them, following the San Francisco *Oracle,* always contain a center spread of poems printed sideways over a color picture of a pair of the local citizens in yab yum or a couple of oral erotic psychodelic dragons or such like. There's only one trouble with this. It makes the poems practically impossible to read, just like you can't hear the words in the rock concerts. Poets who appear in the underground press never seem to publish anywhere else. They are part of the democratization of art, like the innumerable poetry readings, which, whatever the value of the present work, in the final analysis is what is most significant in the culture of the alternative society.

One of the most puzzling things is the absolute indifference to poetry on the part of the second and third generations (counting backwards) of the hip magazines. *Esquire* and its Pantagruelian child *Playboy* may have published a poem or two sometime but if so I never noticed it, yet the targets of both magazines are now people who grew up in social circles of juvenile semi-secession and cynical conformity (something like Kentucky or Missouri in the Civil War) in which poetry was important. I can't understand magazines which devote articles to John Handy III and Albert Ayler, or Kenneth Anger and Stan Brakhage, or The Doors and The Mothers of Invention, but who never publish poetry or even review it. Don't they know those gatefolds read Lenore Kandel?

With such a tremendous burst of creativity over so wide a range of tastes it would be quite impossible to give an adequate bibliography of interesting poetry published since 1965. Here is a list of some of the anthologies which include new poets issued in 1969 alone.

Anania, Michael. *New Poetry Anthology I.* Chicago, The Swallow Press.

Berg, Stephen, and Mezey, Robert. *Naked Poetry.* New York, Bobbs Merrill.

Carroll, Paul. *The Young American Poets.* Chicago and New York, Follett (1968).

Lowenfels, Walter. *The Writing on the Wall.* New York, Doubleday.

Jones, LeRoi, and Neal, Larry. *Black Fire.* New York, Morrow (1968).

Major, Clarence. *The New Black Poetry.* New York, International Publishers.

Pearson, Normal Holmes, *Decade: A Collection of Poems from the First Ten Years of the Wesleyan Poetry Program.* Middletown, Wesleyan University Press.

Schreiber, Ron. *31 New American Poets.* New York, Hill and Wang.

Shuman, R. Baird. *Nine Black Poets.* Durham, Moore Publishing Company (1968).

Solt, Mary Ellen. *Concrete Poetry: A World View.* Bloomington and London, Indiana University Press (1968).

Strand, Mark. *The Contemporary American Poets: American Poetry Since 1940.* New York and Cleveland, World.

Waldman, Anne. *The World Anthology: Poems from the*

St. Marks Poetry Project. Indianapolis and New York, Bobbs Merrill.

Williams, Emmett. *Anthology of Concrete Poetry*. New York, Villefranche and Frankfurt: Something Else Press (1967).

1970

15.
Facing Extinction

I.

In July of 1969 I took part in a poetry reading at Nourse Auditorium—a benefit for the Planning and Conservation League. A goodly number of the city's leading poets read and the auditorium was comfortably full. What was impressive was the immediate spontaneous response to the very name of the organization, of which before most of tlie audiencc and participants had never heard. Equally impressive was the character of the audience. They were like the people who came to the historic readings in The Six Gallery in 1955–56 and the one in Fugazi Hall almost ten years later. It was as though the freaked-out generation had never been, as though the Flower Children had never been sold down the river by the Mafia. I do not mean that the people were all that old. Most of them were as young or younger than those you see making out in the gutter on Haight Street. These people were not victims. They gave every indication of being able to manage their own lives in terms of the values of the alternative society. They had all shown up at the call of conservation because they knew what the other alternative, the dominant society, was all about.

Extinction.

This is the most significant development in the counter-culture. The teeny-boppers may still be in revolt against their fathers and mothers. Elderly half-crazy novelists may still be organizing centers all over Europe to sell society on free heroin. The Underground Press may be full of nakeds, record ads, dope gossip, and comic pornographic personals, but the interest of the counter-culture has shifted to the most important issue in human history. We are becoming extinct. Extinct has become an active verb with a reflexive—*s'extincter*. The dominant society is extincting itself along with everything else it can extinct and especially us. Perfectly calm and collected scientists now say that it is unlikely that the human race will last into the next century and that in the next five or ten years there will begin a series of catastrophic famines in each of which hundreds of millions will die. There are thousands of other species of sentient beings who will go out with man. The possibilities of reversing this process are exceedingly remote and if measures of salvation were put into effect now, this week, most of them would not begin to pay off for a generation.

Japanese birth-control specialists estimate that as effective a program as theirs will take thirty years really to make a difference. The poisoning of the sea and the pollution of inland waters is only beginning. Most of the DDT that has already extincted several species is still in the soil and will be washing into the sea for years even if the use of DDT is given up tomorrow. Most of the high prairie and the intermountain grazing areas have already been destroyed. Twenty years ago demographers looked forward with horror to three billion people in the year 2000. There are now 3½ billion people alive.

Civilization, and not just Western civilization, shows all the symptoms of ever-acclerating breakdown. If "civilization" means the control of life to insure steadily increasing experience of values in intensity, scope, and depth, civilization is not breaking down, it came to an end in August 1914. Man has lost control.

What is accelerating is not the breakdown of civilization, but the breakdown of the species as such. Unless the processes now operating are reversed, and when reversed, are still able to win out, man is a failure. The species has failed. Unfortunately man is not one of those funny-looking rhinoceros-like creatures in the paleontology books whose passing will not make a great deal of difference to other beings. Man has not just been crowded out of his ecological niche; he has destroyed everbody's ecology. The changes which have taken place already in this generation are greater than those postulated to account for the extinction of the dinosaurs.

Nothing more significant has happened recently, and that includes the trip to the moon, than the discovery of the ecological revolution by the youth revolt, the counter-culture. When George Kennan a few years ago in a rather foxy grandpa book told the youth revolt that they have their priorities wrong and that the destruction of the planet was more important than the laws against marihuana everybody said he was a square. Now ever larger numbers of young people are beginning to agree. It's not just that the oldies want to take them out and murder them in a marsh in Southeast Asia; they're busy poisoning them at breakfast here at home and the majority of the people in the world have little breakfast or none. The Bodhisattva's vow is "I will not enter Nirvana until all sentient creatures have been saved." If the alternative society becomes a society of ecological Bodhisattvas we will have reached the final confrontation—mutual aid and respect for life, full awareness of one's place in the community of creatures—these are the foundations for an alternative society. Here are the objectives, the self-discipline, the understanding which can create a purposeful challenge to the murderous dominant society.

Can the youth revolt, now that it is finding out what it is most important of all to revolt against, make a significant difference? It can try. At least in the struggle to live a balanced life of mutual aid, of symbiosis with all the other creatures on earth, it can find the objectives, the hierarchy of life values, and the sources of self-discipline which it has lacked. In doing so it will create an actual, integral counter-culture, a community of health within the Great Sickness, a New Moral World, as

Robert Owen called his community. If we can achieve an ecological morality we will have achieved a community based on Kropotkin's Mutual Aid, and Schweitzer's repect for life, and at the same time a spiritual morality and a community ethic with readily verifiable scientific foundation and with applications and consequences as detailed in the specific day-to-day acts and relations as can be found in any twelve-volume work of casuistry and moral theology. The applications will be most always quite obvious and will not need a Talmud or a casuistry. Can this happen? There is everything against it. The Dutch royal family, the duPonts, the Rockefellers drench the world with poisons. The Black militants raid family-planning offices in the ghettos and beat up the workers. The head of the birth-control plan in India proposes to solve the problem with a year of national abstinence. The Pope says if you take the pill you'll go to hell.

If poets like Gary Snyder, Michael McClure, Richard Brautigan, David Meltzer, Ron Loewinsohn, Lew Welch, and the rest and their audiences preach and practice the ecological revolution, they're not likely to win; the time is gone, but at least they can establish a Kingdom in the face of Apocalypse, a garrisoned society of the morally responsible which will face extinction with clean consciences and lives as happily lived as possible.

In the past men have planned utopias where life would be better and they have advocated revolution to get rid of the predatory masters of society and bring about a world where man was no longer wolf to man. Meanwhile the human race struggled on, crippled and thwarted by exploitation and its side effects, from alcoholism to silicosis, but it survived. For the last two hundred years we have seen the growth of an economic and social system based fundamentally on the extractive industries and with a built-in dynamism in its mode of production that forces it into ever-increasing production at all costs. This competitive system has universalized amorality based on covetousness. For the last fifty years the benefits, such as they are, of this system have gradually been extended to most of the productive workers of the major industrial countries—the "metropoles." This is least true of the United States where about a tenth of the population is redundant, youth, the aged, Negroes, Southern poor whites and others. This is not due to the backwardness of the American economy; quite the contrary. We have just gone through a long boom period with ever-accumulating surpluses; yet the over-all production has never passed 80 per cent of capacity. The source of profit is no longer, as it was in Marx's day, labor power. Every year we need fewer people to produce more. The surplus we lock up in subsidized housing projects or Aid to Dependent Children or in Garrison State College, or toss in the disposall of Vietnam. Our social-economic structure is itself in a state of civil war. The old extractive-industrial-financial structure based ultimately on the exploitation of labor power applied directly to primary raw materials is at war with the new technological society of computers and transistors and the Keynesian morality of Hugh Hefner's *la vie luxueuse*. Meanwhile outside the metropoles starvation, disorder, breakdown sweep over the southern three-quarters of the globe.

Twenty-five years ago all the contradictions and conflicts of the present had already come into existence but they only threatened men individually with war, hunger, and crippled lives. Today an extractive accumulative society does not just threaten, but makes certain the extinction of the human species within a comparatively short time. The carbon-dioxide content of the atmosphere can no longer be kept in balance even over the equatorial regions. A dense fog of carcinogens blankets not single cities but whole areas, the Rhine-Saar, the Upper Po, the Bay of Naples, the Tokyo-Osaka-Nagasaki metropolitan complexes as well of course as the major cities. I have crossed the Siskiyus at 25,000 feet and seen the smog filling the entire Central Valley of California and I have seen it rise on the warm morning air from around Milan and cover Lake Como in the Alps. Lake Erie is a cesspool. Lake Michigan is unfit for swimming at Milwaukee and Chicago and stinks all summer long so that the grand rich are now abandoning their lakeside stately homes to charitable institutions, dance seminars, and apocalyptic Black religious groups. If all the atomic-energy installations now planned are installed they will raise the temperatures of the oceans with cataclysmic results. The things we are doing to our environment are changing it far more drastically than the changes necessary to account for the extinction of the great reptiles at the end of the Jurassic Age and incomparably more quickly.

I have quoted before the old-time, now-abandoned slogan of the U.S. Forest Service, "The forest is a crop, not a mine." Unless we can stop treating the planet as a mine and start treating it as a crop, people now living will see the beginning of the end of the human species.

Not only are we destroying the ecology outside us that makes human life possible, we have passed the saturation point of human, interpersonal ecology. We are already doing all those things those overcrowded rats in the laboratory did, no matter how well-fed and cared for they were. As everybody recognized when they read about the experiments in the papers—except the Pope.

What can we do about it? Probably very little. Because the old order is shutting down with a police state. In the Thirties the Marxists called Fascism and Nazism "forced rationalization" of the German and Italian economies (Lenin admitted that Bolshevism was precisely forced rationalization). Today the state, but most especially the American state, is dedicated to forced irrationalization. Unless this can be halted there is literally no hope for the human race. But what does this mean? It means de-mounting the whole structure, rebuilding it, and starting off in the opposite direction. Growth rates and GNP's and capital expansion have got to be replaced by de-accumulation, by changing the standard-of-living value systems so that the possession of large numbers of commodities becomes a vice, not a virtue. The extractive industries must be reduced to a minimum —today scrap iron of the highest quality is a drug on the market. The use of fossil fuels as at present must be brought to a complete stop. Coal, oil, and gas should be consumed totally with nothing but completely inert residues at the sites and sent out over wires. Atomic plants should be stopped until someone can figure out how to destroy the wastes. More and more articles should be made of organic plastics from sources that can be grown. Chemical fertilizers and insecticides must be replaced by organic manures which now pollute all our bodies of water instead of being pumped into the fields and by the ecological management of the health of agricultural crops. For instance, replacing poison sprays with ladybird beetles. Along with this would have to go a complete moral conversion from the acquisitive, competitive, covetous "virtues" of present society to a whole new scale of cooperative mutual aid, a simplicity value system not unlike that of the South Sea Islanders of Romance. The population growth must not just be stopped, but reversed. The optimum is probably about one billion people to the planet.

You say this sounds like turning the whole world into a national park? Precisely. We must save ourselves as we are trying to save the sandhill crane.

II.

Santa Barbara city, county, and university certainly represent in practically pure form what a Marxist would call a democratic dictatorship of the white Anglo-Saxon Protestant upper middle class. This of course is true of most communities in America—or of a dozen other countries as well. But not in so pure and protected a form. In the old days Santa Barbara, like Pasadena or Piedmont, Atherton or Hillsborough, walled itself off from the destructive boom exploitation that started to ruin California from the very beginning. It was the prettiest town in the state on a site as beautiful as Naples, Hong Kong, or San Francisco, and it intended to remain that way. We forget, if we ever knew, for we are certainly not taught about it in school, how deeply rooted the economic morality of the extractive industries is in California's history. Mining, lumber, and oil—get yours and get out and to hell with the consequences—but this was true of Spanish California. Cattle were turned loose to run wild and were not rounded up but shot on the range. The hides and suet were stripped off and carried to port on pack horses. The carcasses were poisoned and left to "destroy the vermin." Every summer the savannahs were burned off "to improve the range." The fires also served to round up and trap the Indians who were shot down as they fled from the enclosing flames very much as in a west Kansas jackrabbit hunt. The Americans drove sheep through the higher mountains and pigs through the lower. These practices led to a complete change in the biota of the state. The highly nutritious bunch grass and other perennial grasses vanished to be replaced by grass weeds, especially Spanish wild oat. The condor, the grizzly, once extremely common, became extinct or survived in only a very few individuals. The last California grizzly was killed at Horse Corral Meadow in Kings Canyon Park a generation ago. A half-grizzly, half-black bear drowsed away his old age in one of the bear pits back of the Academy of Sciences in Golden Gate Park about forty years ago. The tiny condor reservation is unlikely to survive poachers and the effects of DDT on eggshells for more than five or ten more years. Sierra meadows once looked like lakes when the camass with its blue flowers and highly nutritious bulbs was in bloom. The pigs exterminated the camass in all but a very few remote meadows. It was in these very years that Karl Marx said that Europe survived only due to the humane traditions of an older culture. "If you want to see capitalism in all its horror," said Marx, "go to California."

Santa Barbara was a little enclave of comparative sanity in the midst of wholesale destruction. During World War II exploitation was unbridled and ran wild everywhere. Some of the finest timber in California was logged off and shipped to Indonesia to make corduroy roads through the jungles—where of course more suitable trees had to be cut down to clear the road itself. Then the armed forces decided to move everything by air and many of these roads were never used. This is an example of the kind of devastation that began to lap at the carefully protected walls of Santa Barbara. The city has been overbuilt and many of the old controls are gone. Outside the city limits whole towns have sprung up subject only to county control and built-in areas certain to be flooded or burned over within comparatively short periods. The oil disaster woke up the community. Ruthless exploitation of an unneeded natural resource, heavily subsidized by the Federal Government, now threatens to destroy the very meaning of Santa Barbara. Perhaps the oil leak, which is not stopped, but still flows merrily on and apparently cannot be stopped, has brought home to the highly protected WASP rich the nature of the exploitations from which they draw dividends. It may well be that this catastrophe will tip the scales and that a rigorously planned and coordinated community can be re-created.

As for the university. It should have been limited in size to its population of five years ago. Its growth should certainly be stopped now. Students, junior faculty, and the enlightened members of the administration must be free from the veto powers of people who came here to take their doctor's degrees years ago and said, "What a nice place to retire," and proceeded to do so. Communication has to be opened up with all the most advanced tendencies in education all over the world so that both the progressive faculty and administration people and the student movements, Black or white, have the essential information before they can even know what they want or how to solve their problem. That information is not available now. There is nothing unusual, for instance, about the way I conduct my classes. There are plenty like them, not just at Bard or Reed, but at Harvard or NYU. The only group in constant contact with its fellows elsewhere is the leadership of the Black Students' Union, but most of the rank-and-file members are still unaware of what's going on in the movement elsewhere.

As for the student residents' ghetto, Isla Vista, that is hopeless. It should be condemned, torn down, and started over along the lines once hoped for by the idealists. This means a publicly owned and operated renewal plan which would create a *cité universitaire* of beautiful buildings, good dining halls, and restaurants, with theaters, coffee shops, bookshops, and plenty of places for recreation, all set in the midst of wide lawns and plenty of trees, with a maximum landscaping use of the beaches and the views out to the sea and the islands. Why not turn the whole thing over to Ian McHarg and Louis Kahn? Of the greatest importance again is the opening up of communications with the outside world. There is scarcely a literate magazine in any language from anywhere in the world that you can't buy on Telegraph Avenue or around Harvard Square. The one magazine stand in Isla Vista carries cheesecake and surfer magazines and got in trouble over ZAP Comics, and the magazine stand in the university bookshop is considerably below the level of the one in the Fort Dodge airport or a Wichita Falls drugstore.

Fundamental to the whole conflict in education is the necessity for a real change of heart. The academic hack must be pushed in the background and deprived of veto power. In the worldwide crisis of the human spirit there is no room in education for anyone but enthusiastically dedicated pedagogues, a word ironically enough the hacks have made a term of abuse. With the onset of a fully developed technological society it has now become possible to attack human self-alienation head on. The alienation of man from his work, from his fellows, and from himself can be done away with by the end of the century. Instead, in Russia or East Germany, as much or even more than in the United States, France, or England, alienation is increasing like a deadly pandemic. The May Days in Paris, the complete shutdown of the educational system in Japan in the Spring of 1969, are symptoms of a worldwide social disease, a new Black Death. What the education system should be doing is developing in the communities that it can create within itself—*de-alienators,* thousands and thousands of young people who can go out into the world their elders are destroying and overcome the social morality of *homo homini lupus.* Every classroom, whether in projective geometry, Assyriology, or literature, should be tested by its capacity for *agape*—creative interpersonal respect and affection. This is what we mean by the absolute necessity for revolution in education. Is it likely to take place? No.

Meanwhile they plan to destroy the lagoon betwen UCSB and the mainland with a freeway designed to handle so large a volume of traffic that it would be necessary completely to cover with concrete both Isla Vista and the university site to take care of the parked cars.

III

Of the many demands of concerned students and faculty at the University of California, Santa Barbara, there is not one that cannot be met, usually right now. What are they? All you have to do is circulate around and ask. These are not my ideas, but put together they form a definite emergency program, which once implemented in totality, would make it possible to commence to begin to start moving towards a human, humane, humanistic, humanitarian educational environment and interpersonal relations:

"Stop the Vietnam War immediately, and totally, and withdraw from the country as fast as possible, and if it's necessary, mobilize all the world's passenger ships and reactivate the World War II old cans still lying at anchor in the bays on both coasts. The airlines do something like that every year for the pilgrimage to Mecca. It's no problem."

"Legalize grass. Even the square squares who say it's harmful have to admit that it's far less harmful than alcohol or cigarettes. Once the convivial weed that practically everybody under forty uses now is made socially harmless by being decriminalized, then we can start by individual group action to stamp out the killers —speed and smack—and purge the Mafia from the community. Of course, everybody knows grass is illegal for no other reason than that the government can't tax it, and the Mafia can't control it."

"Stop immediately all military research on all campuses."

"Provide the pill to all who ask for it from the University Health Service."

"Reduce the enrollment by 5 per cent a year for four years (let them build other small universities elsewhere)."

"Allow only service automobile traffic on the campus and in Isla Vista. Demolish the parking lots and plant them again with trees and grass. Put sufficient parking buildings on the landward side of the Slough, where otherwise an industrial slum is bound to grow up. Provide free public transportation from the parking buildings to IV and UCSB, and free bicycles. The cheapest and best way to do this would be with a four-lane, four-speed belt. They move iron ore that way for over a hundred miles in Queensland and Brazil."

"Condemn and demolish Isla Vista, and build a *cité universitaire* with the best possible architects and landscapists, a publicly owned and operated renewal plan of beautiful buildings.

"Break up the school into colleges, not by professions, or departments, but with salubrious lounges and dining halls in which people with the widest variety of interest can mingle on a fraternal basis as they do, or did, in the colleges at Oxford and Cambridge, or in an ideal Greek letter house. For those that want them there should be a Malcolm X College, and a Zapata College. Oriental students do not seem to desire such, but if they do, they should be provided."

"Create a department of Ethnic Studies for Whites—WASP Remedial Education—to teach the upper-middle-class social illiterates from the high schools of Southern California's suburbia how to get along with other Americans."

"Permit nude bathing on the beaches and in the pools, and move towards the introduction of nude physical education. Build more recreational pools—one for each college."

"Establish appointment review and, separately, curriculum review councils in each department which will include every step on the academic ladder from the senior faculty to freshmen. Grant immediately the demands of the junior faculty, T.A.'s, and graduates for effective roles in faculty life where now they are second-class citizens at best, and indentured servants in the lower echelons."

"Stop fussing about the Faculty Club. Everybody should have places like the Faculty Club where folks can relax, read, talk together, and socialize. Stop fussing about soul food in the cafeteria. The first thing to get is just edible food. Evening meals in the commons of the college should be accompanied with table wines or beer for those that want it. Sure it's against the law. Change the law. Practically everything is against the law. It's really true that there are married people in prisons all over the United States serving long sentences for practicing oral sex with their spouses. Most all laws need to be repealed, so we can start over with social regulations that make sense."

"No grades. Make all courses pass - fail."

"No actual classes larger than thirty. Mass lectures could be unlimited in size and open to anybody who wishes to come in but they should be divorced completely from the teaching process, a totally different and antagonistic activity. This is the ancient European system and what the word 'university' really means."

"Abolish the use of the Title of Honor, 'doctor.' In America it is the height of bad manners to call anyone but a medical man doctor. Nobody calls the other folks 'master' or 'bachelor.'

If a student calls you doctor, tell him to take two aspirin and a hot bath and call you in the morning."

"There are tons of government money available for fellowships, travel grants, and individual projects, especially for upper-division and M.A. candidate people. They are kept a profound secret because they would drain off those indentured servants titled T.A.'s but called by the more depraved senior faculty, 'warm bodies.' Grants and fellowships should not only be widely publicized, they should be urged on students, and there should be a well-functioning office of people highly trained—and it sure takes high training—in writing up foundation and government grant applications which must be in a language resembling the interbreeding of Etruscan and Tlinkit."

"Midterms should be true 'tests'—is the experiment fulfilling the hypothesis? They should be uninhibited raps, evaluations of student-teacher relations and course relevance."

"Abolish the quarter system. Even the semester system is absurd. It takes months even to start a class into a subject and to establish the community necessary for the educative relationship to begin. This is certainly true of the graduates of Southern California upper-middle-class slurburbia so desperately in need of remedial education."

"No student can begin to learn until he has mastered the meaning of Cohn-Bendit's slogan that launched the Paris May Days—'When examined, answer with questions.' "

These are not my suggestions, as I have said before, but turned up by questioning a wide variety of the socially literate faculty and students. They all add up to one total—a massive effort to destroy forever, not by riot and violence but by mutual responsibility, the custodian-inmate, faculty-student relationship. Students should stop calling themselves and not let anybody else call them kids. Alexander the Great and Sir Philip Sydney were dead before they were as old as many students today. Challenge depersonalization in the classroom. Teachers, don't let your students treat you like a turnkey. Students, insist that you not be treated as a child. There is only one kind of authority that is not exploitation or indifferent contempt, and that is *responsibility*. Responsibility is a two-way relationship and so is the authority it engenders.

A properly raised child of six has authority vis-à-vis its parents to the limits of its responsibility within the family. This is the copesitic. Until the university gets rid of the German, authoritarian *Wissenschaft* structure of pseudo-scholarship and returns to the ancient tradition of the collegiate family, things will get worse and worse until there is nothing left but burned-out buildings and youth in work camps or off at war.

Mutual affection, respect, interest, loyalty, and simple physical touch—*agape,* the love of comrades in a spiritual adventure. This is what the educational relationship should be. If it isn't, it isn't education. Nothing could indicate better the alienation of what the head of the English department at another university calls the crocodiles in the back bays of tenure, than the Good Gray Doktor at another school who once asked me, "How do you enforce discipline with theories like yours?" "I don't." "But who is responsible?" "We all are." "I can't understand that. What is the principle behind it?" "I would say, *agape.*" I could see his mind running over the index to Krafft-Ebing's *Psychopathia Sexualis* which he doubtless knew by heart, unable to locate the word between aberrations and annilinctus. "But just how do you do it?" said he. "Like a kind of dedicated, even ecstatic, underground mass culminating with the kiss of peace and communion." During the rest of the brief conversation I realized that he thought I meant a black mass. A man who would believe such a thing or believe anybody could get away with it, or that students would accept it, has spent his entire life at the bottom of an abandoned missile silo. When I told my students (as an example of utter alienation), one of the girls said, "Well, we might as well be hung for wolves as dogs; I'll take off my clothes and get up on the table." Another said, "I'll make a psychedelic chasuble, ornamented with bats and rattlesnakes." Another said, "I'll bring some incense mixed with hash and opium and we can invite all the lost souls embalmed in tenure." I guess we didn't feel all that self-sacrificing because somehow we never got around to it. Too busy writing songs much like Abelard, Aquinas, or the *Carmina Burana.*

1968–1969